Life on Insulin

A Memoir

Andrew J. Schreier

LifeRich Publishing is a registered trademark of
The Reader's Digest Association, Inc.

LifeRich Publishing books may be ordered through booksellers or by contacting:

LifeRich Publishing
1663 Liberty Drive
Bloomington, IN 47403
www.liferichpublishing.com
1 (888) 238-8637

ISBN: 978-1-4897-0502-0 (sc)
ISBN: 978-1-4897-0503-7 (e)

Library of Congress Control Number: 2015911717

Print information available on the last page.

LifeRich Publishing rev. date: 08/03/2015

Dedication

This book is dedicated to everyone who always
believed in me - - because without you
this story would be drastically different.

To all those who struggle - - anything
is possible for those who believe in the
power of dreaming and changing.

Epigraph

"One of the greatest gifts in life is the ability to have the courage to share our story with the rest of the world."

Andrew J. Schreier

CHAPTER 1

Death is Knocking

*"While I thought that I was learning how
to live, I have been learning how to die."*

Quote Inspired by Leonardo da Vinci

A pancreas. Just one of the many parts of the human body. Not one of those parts we talk about a lot or focus on taking care of like the heart, brain, lungs, and so forth. But, a pancreas? A body part that did its job and no one needs to know anything more about it. If you were to ask me how important my pancreas was back then, I don't even know if it would have broken the top of the list. Why would it? It meant nothing to me as long as it was working. But, when it completely stopped my world change beyond anything I could ever have imagined. Before I could appreciate what my pancreas did my life was going to have to go on without it.

Before this day happened my story was nothing unique or special to tell. I was a young, energetic kid living a life that was pretty usual among most people I knew. Most of the time, I was just being a child with minimal responsibilities and most importantly running around with as much of a carefree attitude as possible. What adult life would

I imagine having to experience at the age of twelve? Why would I think something would come along and drastically change all that?

That something did happen. It occurred out of nowhere; without any heads up or warning signs to give any kind of clue whatsoever that life as I knew it was about to change. You wake up thinking that today is going to be like every other day. Then life decides to shake things up and turn your life around into an entirely different direction that you could never have anticipated.

It's easier to reflect back on it now and see how the story unfolded, but at the time its purpose and meaning was nowhere in sight. I didn't grasp the importance of having this happen to me until years later and after many unfortunate events occurred along the way. Now, this serves as the story of how something entered my life and created nothing but complete devastation and then in the end left me with ultimate inspiration.

Babysitting my younger cousin is never a hassle. We get along great, and there are never any problems when I watch her. Being twelve years old and babysitting kind of puts a little chip on your shoulder that you are now responsible enough to start to have adult-like responsibilities. Becoming a babysitter is not something I was looking forward to as a career, but let's face it I was young and it was something convenient to do to make easy money.

It is about time to head over to my aunt and uncle's house, so I grab my empty school bag and yell to my father to hurry up. We stop at the local grocery store before it is time to report for duty. I run in real quick and grab two small cartons of chocolate milk. As soon as I get back to the car I put the two milks in my empty school bag, and we are ready to go.

The usual routine takes place throughout the night. We watch television and spend all of our time in the living room. Within minutes of being there I begin to have this craving for something to drink. Immediately, I open my school bag and quickly grab the first milk. I consume the whole carton at once. I thought drinking the milk would instantaneously quench my thirst, but it doesn't. In fact, the craving to drink somehow grows stronger.

Without hesitation, I grab the second milk and drink it faster than the first one. The same response happens, and the thirst refuses to be settled. Seconds after drinking the second milk I vomit all over the floor. I feel sorry for my cousin because she has to witness it all, but I am more worried about what is happening to me. Before going over to babysit everything felt fine. There was nothing wrong, and now I can't even begin to imagine what is causing this strange reaction.

I start to worry. Here I am watching out for my younger cousin, and I am starting to get sick. All of the sudden I am relieved to hear the garage door open. The kitchen door opens, and I notice my older cousin walking through the kitchen and into the living room. Going home becomes the first thought to enter my mind as the thirst is not getting any better. We gather my belongings and she drives me home immediately.

The next three days became such a blur as my mind kept going in and out. I spend the entire time lying on the family room couch, vomiting any substance I consume. The first two days are identical. My family cannot think of any other explanation and assume I simply have the flu. What reason would we have to think otherwise? Usually when I come down with any illness, the recovery process consists of resting, drinking liquids, and watching movies.

It doesn't take too long for me to realize something is seriously wrong with my health. The first two days I consistently drink eight-ounce glasses of milk. After every glass I consume I vomit almost on the spot. The vomiting and discomfort don't stop me though. The thirst is so strong that it feels as if I am going to suffocate if I don't drink something. I continue to drink glass after glass and end up vomiting.

The uncontrollable thirst is too strong to handle. I can't remember the last time, or any time for that matter, where my appetite to consume liquids felt so intense. In the first two days, I drink over two gallons of milk and throw all of it up. My parents and I come to the conclusion that the milk is upsetting my stomach. The next day we decide I should only drink water. As much as I do not like the idea of not being able to consume milk, I am okay with drinking water if that makes the vomiting go away.

Both parents head off to work again in hopes that drinking water will ease the vomiting and discomfort. Before they leave my mom brings me a large cup of water. I try to be tough and act like the thirst isn't bothering me as much. When she hands me the water, I place it on the ground at first to make it seem like they shouldn't worry. As soon as they leave I reach for the cup of water as fast as I can. After my first drink, I vomit all over the floor. I start to panic because I know throwing up water means something is seriously wrong.

I begin to ask questions inside my head. *What is going on? What is happening to me? Why am I throwing up water? What kind of flu is this? How am I not getting better by now?* I feel weak. I feel sick. I am scared, and I am worried. Worst of all, I am alone. The panic inside grows stronger because I have no idea what is going on. I drink another glass of water and throw it all up. I sit on the couch, motionless and start to feel incredibly weak to the point where I am not moving. I need to do something about it.

Immediately, I attempt to get up and call my mom at work. I can't move and my body feels like all the energy inside of it is completely drained. My panic level increases because I cannot move and am not capable of getting help. I lose track of time. It feels like it has been forever, but I honestly don't have a clue. I hear a noise in our driveway. The garage door opens and I can hear a car pulling in. The door to the house opens next and I can hear my mom's work shoes hit the hardwood floor. Right away, she calls out my name. I can hear her put her keys on our kitchen counter. She calls my name again, but there is no response. Nothing comes out of my mouth. I am trying to talk to her, but none of the thoughts are verbalized. I am screaming for help inside my head.

Mom, I am right here. Come quick!

Nothing comes out though. I cannot speak, and I am the only one who knows I am screaming. My mother calls out for me again.

Please come quickly!! I need help!!

Again, my mom calls out, and there is silence. All of the sudden my head is spinning and before I know it...

DARKNESS. I blackout out before my mother even gets to me.

My mother walks through the kitchen and comes around the corner to where I am laying on the couch. My eyes open out of the darkness, and she is kneeling right beside me. I am relieved to see her, but it quickly turns into feelings of panic again. As she looks into my eyes, I can see her face turn entirely pale as if she has seen a ghost. All of the sudden my vision gets blurry again and before I know it...

DARKNESS. When my eyes open again I feel my mom struggling to put a Wisconsin Badgers sweatshirt over my shoulders. She picks me up and takes me to the garage and places me in the backseat of the car. Thoughts aren't even making sense in my head. Sentences aren't forming and before she lays me down my mind shuts off.

DARKNESS again. I manage to open my eyes again. She is now carrying me through two automatic doors that read Emergency Room in bright red. My head continues to spin, vision is blurry, and before I know it I am unconscious. I wake up for a few moments, which feels like just a number of seconds, and I feel nurses pulling off my sweatshirt and appearing to take care of me in the hospital. All of the sudden...

DARKNESS. I open my eyes, and I am lying down in an ambulance. I have no clue as to how long I have been here or what the doctors or nurses have said about my condition. I can look through the small window in the ambulance and notice we are driving away from the hospital heading in the other direction. *Why are we leaving?* For the last time, my head is spinning, my vision turns pitch black and I am unconscious. The next time I wake up I am lying in a hospital bed.

As I wake up, I feel nurses and doctors surrounding me. Their hands are all over me scrambling to do a variety of things that I can barely understand. I am being poked and stabbed with various devices, with all sorts of instruments attached to me. All of the nurses are describing what they are doing. One is talking about the intravenous lines going through my arms. Another is explaining how much insulin is being administered. One nurse at the end of the bed is trying to poke my feet, but I cannot feel a thing. I want to be left alone. I feel weird. I feel disgusting. I want them to leave. I desperately wish for a second that I could black out again. Soon enough, I close my eyes, and the darkness settles in.

As I wake up, I am laying in a hospital bed. I have no idea what has happened. I remember the nurses poking and prodding at me and describing all of this medical terminology that I didn't understand. The aches and pains are constant, and making matters worse I still can't move. I try speaking but I am unable to get any words out. I look down at my motionless body. As I look down, I notice monitors taped onto my chest. Looking at my arms I see two intravenous lines piercing into my skin. My feet are bare with a cold feeling to the touch.

I have no idea what's going on, where I am, or what happened to me. I look to my left and see my mother sitting in a hospital chair. She has the saddest look on her face. Tears are slowly rolling down her face, and she is sitting there completely motionless. I see some movement when she moves her hand to wipe one of the tears away. She sits there completely silent, and I can't imagine what it is like for her to see her son in this condition. I desperately want to ask her what happened and to find some safety in all this discomfort, but seeing her like that makes it difficult for me to say anything - so I don't.

I want to get up and go over to her. I want to wrap my arms around her and tell her everything is okay, even though I don't know if I am or not. I want to tell her to stop crying and apologize for what is going on. I can't though. I can only sit here. I am entirely drained of energy, with medical equipment attached to me, and still cannot speak. I can only sit here.

All I want to do is lie in this hospital bed and fall asleep. I want to wake up and realize all of this was some horrible nightmare. These are the moments we would rather accept having the nightmare than realizing everything that happened is now a reality. With everything going on, I wasn't sure if it was real or in fact the worst nightmare I have ever had. All of the going in and out of consciousness the last day makes it difficult to get a grasp of anything.

All I know is that sitting here in the hospital bed is the most discomfort I can ever recall experiencing. I feel disgusting. I feel dirty. What is most concerning is that I still have no idea what is going on. No explanation, no reason, and no solution for what will happen in the future. *Why is this happening to me?* I close my eyes and feel comfort in the darkness. The reality of the situation is getting pretty scary now so closing my eyes and falling back asleep seems the better of the two options. As soon as I start to fall asleep and wish this could all be a nightmare, a nurse comes in through the door and explains the doctor will be coming in momentarily.

CHAPTER 2

A Recovering Diabetic

"Recovery begins from the darkest moment."

Quote Inspired by John Major

The doctor comes into the room and stands beside the hospital bed. He looks at my mother first with this sad expression on his face. I am anxious to hear what he is going to say. At this point, I have gotten little information about the entire situation. Nurses were talking about insulin, blood sugar levels, intravenous lines, heart monitors, and a bunch of other medical information that was irrelevant to me. Talking to the doctor is the first chance I get to learn about the truth of what occurred.

The doctor clears his throat and says, "You are being diagnosed with juvenile diabetes."

I can't physically talk, so everything I say circulates only in my mind. *What is juvenile diabetes?*

As soon as I hear those two words I freeze. My mind starts to go through a hundred different questions in a compulsive, repetitive manner. So many questions are going through my head to the point I start blocking what the doctor is saying. Those two words are the only words I can remember him saying.

Questions are pouring in and out. *What is juvenile diabetes? What does that even mean? Does my father know? Where are my brother and sister? Is juvenile diabetes contagious? Do I have to get shots? Is there a cure for juvenile diabetes? What is my life going to be like now that I have juvenile diabetes? Could this end up killing me? Does any of friends know? Any of my friends here?* The questions never stop coming.

I only have the faintest idea of what juvenile diabetes is. I never learned about it and was never informed about the condition. The only information I know is the fact that my body no longer produces natural insulin, which is used to break down all the sugar I eat. *Does this mean I can't have any sugar? What am I supposed to eat?*

Along with the diagnosis of diabetes I have acquired thrush. Absolutely no clue what thrush is either. It is on my tongue, and it feels dirty. It feels disgusting. And now I feel even more disgusting sitting in this hospital bed with some gross infection sticking to my tongue. The thrush is preventing me from talking, and I have no idea when it is going to go away.

As I lay in the hospital bed day after day, feeling bedridden and sick, I think about walking over to the window and jumping out of it. I think committing suicide I can end the pain immediately. I can't even get up to walk over to the window. These thoughts are driven purely by frustration, concern, worry, and most notably fear. Life was entirely different just days before this occurred. I was running around and going to school like a normal child with no real worries. Now, I'm sitting in a hospital bed with some diagnosis that is entirely new to understand.

Juvenile diabetes is a new mystery for me to try and solve. No family members are diabetic. No close friends have the disease either. I feel all alone. I feel different already because I don't even know who to go to about what has just happened. If I could just go home, maybe it would make things better. But no, I am not allowed to leave the hospital room let alone the entire hospital itself.

No one explains anything about the condition of the diabetes. I am clueless, and I feel lost. I already hate it because I don't know what it is. That's how I feel about being diagnosed with diabetes. Look what it has done to me already in a few days and I'm supposed to live with this for the rest of my life? I am left having no clue about what it really is and the impact it will have on my life. Without knowing what diabetes is I start automatically hating everything about it.

The mystery of my disease starts because I don't even know what it is. In grade school, I learned about it for ten minutes, and the only two words I remember are 'insulin' and 'sugar.' At this point, I have little knowledge of what juvenile diabetes is and what it can do. More questions continued to pour into my head. *What is this disease and what kind of life do I have now? Why does this have to happen to me?*

The nurse comes in through the door to introduce the first insulin injection, which I soon realize I am dependent on to stay alive. So apparently the body organ responsible for producing insulin decided to up and quit on me. She explains the procedure and discusses how the doctors want newly diagnosed patients with juvenile diabetes to try the injection in the stomach. As soon as the syringe punctures my stomach I moan in pain as loud as I can. The thrush on my tongue is so severe that I can't even yell; so the yelling occurs inside of my head.

AHHHHH! What are you doing to me?

A tear comes rolling down my cheek. The injection is extremely painful because in a three-day period I lost eighteen pounds, and there isn't a lot of fat on my stomach to absorb the injection. *Injecting needles in my stomach is something I am supposed to do every single day? Not just every day but multiple times a day? Do they actually think a twelve-year-old can inject himself repetitively with syringes and poke himself in the fingers throughout the day?* As the nurse finishes up she smiles and says, "That's all you have to do. Easy right?"

I am very new at this, but injecting someone else does seem a lot easier than having to do it to yourself. More anger and frustration settle in with the idea that this is supposed to be easy. The idea of getting used to daily injections and finger pokes appear entirely unrealistic, but deep down the anger and frustrations are there because I am terrified. *What kind of life is this for me? Insulin injections are what I have to do each day in order to keep living? What happens if I can't do it?*

The rest of the recovery time in the hospital is spent watching movies on diabetes, taking thrush medicine, regaining strength and energy, learning how to manage diabetes, and feeling all alone. My older sister is home alone, and my younger brother is staying over at a friend's house. Even though I miss them, I don't want them here. I don't want them to see their brother like this. I am dirty. I feel disgusting. I am weak and sick. Remembering how my mother looked when I woke up and saw her next to the window makes me think I can't see anyone else in my family go through that.

I am sitting here in pain and feeling all alone. I am surrounded by warmth and yet feel so cold. I am surrounded by a loving mother, yet I feel all alone. I feel helpless, even with so much care in my presence. I can't sleep, and the thoughts are persistently running around in my head. All I can do is drive myself insane trying to catch up with them. I have to live with this for the rest of my life, and I honestly have no idea how to do that.

The day turns into night. I sit in the hospital bed thinking about everything going on. I am tired and can't stay up anymore. My eyelids become heavy and start to close slowly. I fall asleep. All of the sudden my eyes open up and my mom is carrying me through two automatic doors that say Emergency Room in bright red. Again, my head is spinning, my vision is blurry, and before I know it...

DARKNESS. I open my eyes, and I am lying down in an ambulance, looking through the windows. Through the small window,

I can see the sign for the hospital at the top of the hill. My head is spinning, and my vision turns pitch black and I am unconscious.

All of the sudden I wake up and am sweating. I look around to see my mother sleeping in a chair by the window. The monitors and intravenous lines are attached, and I realize this was all a bad dream. It felt so genuine as if everything was happening again. I start to cry because I cannot take the pain anymore. Everything felt exactly the same way it did before and the pain went through its vicious cycle again. I don't want my mom to wake up, so I place my hands over my eyes, nose, and mouth and cry into them.

I am twisting and turning all night in this bed. I lay on my side, and it hurts. I sit on the other side, and it hurts. I try and lay on my stomach, and all I can think and feel is the pain caused by that first insulin injection. I flip over and sit on my back, and it is in pain from throwing up. I want to fall asleep and wish that this whole thing could just simply be over. We hope for pleasant dreams and rarely do we wish for the nightmares, but knowing that this is a nightmare would provide relief. Knowing this hell I am living in is not real would be the best thing I could hope for right now.

As I sit here, I start to wonder how long this nightmare will last. As much as I pray for this to be a nightmare I can't be in that much denial. I can feel the pain. I feel my lifeless body. Instead of waking up I am living in my nightmare.

I am afraid to go back asleep. There is no chance I am willing to fall asleep and let the nightmare come into my head once again. So I don't sleep. I don't want to experience the tragic event again and avoiding sleep will at least prevent that from occurring for now. As unpleasant as it is staying awake into the late night hours in a dark hospital bed, the idea of re-experiencing those events again is even more unpleasant.

During the final day of recovery, my mother comes in from the hallway and hands over a package full of cards. The cards are from all of my classmates at school. I feel relieved to know my peers at school were at least made aware of what happened. I am also relieved to know someone notified them of my current condition and progress towards recovery. Most of the cards are very thoughtful. Students drew pictures and had encouraging words of getting better. Most of them expressed sympathy and hope I will return to school having a complete recovery.

Looking through some of the cards makes me feel different than the rest of my classmates. Some students decide to draw pictures of needles, insulin, and sugary foods like candy and donuts. I haven't even seen anyone from school and yet I already feel different from them. I feel disgusting and disease-ridden because of the images some of them have drawn. I don't like feeling this way and all of the sudden the appeal of going back to school quickly diminishes.

The last day in the hospital is hard. The nursing staff doesn't allow me to leave until I eat my entire dinner. I thought, after all the videos and lectures I had been forced to watch the least they could do is let me go. The nurse doesn't have to eat spicy spaghetti with her tongue covered in thrush. The taste is so terrible it takes over an hour to finish the small meal. The only thing on my mind is getting far away from this hospital. I want to leave this place that has brought me the life-changing news.

A wheelchair is brought into the room from the hallway. The loss of eighteen pounds kept me weak and drained of all my energy. The car is running outside the hospital doors. I look all around as they wheel me through the hospital. I see patients who look sick, miserable, dirty, and full of diseases just like I do. I had been to hospitals before and looked at patients like them with sympathy for what they were experiencing. It is different this time because now I am one of those patients.

As my father rolls my wheelchair out the door, I quickly notice my brother and sister sitting in the back of the car. A tear develops in my eye again. It isn't from the physical pain of a syringe or the emotional pain of trying to answer the questions in my head. This tear is a sign of relief and joy to see familiar faces. I love my mother for staying with me in the hospital. I love my father for coming to get me out of this place of pain. I love my siblings for being in the back seat to pick me up. I love them all and I want to go home where I can feel safe and comforted once again. I get in the front seat of the car and finally get to go home after nearly a week stuck in the hospital.

The next couple of weeks at home would be the same exact routine. In the morning, I have to wake up and take my blood sugar level with my glucose monitor. The doctors explain the lancet (also known as a finger poker) used to measure my blood glucose levels feels like a small prick. At times, I can't feel it at all, and other times it feels like my finger is being poked with a sharp pin. The finger pokes leaves calluses on my fingers. The calluses make me feel more insecure about my condition.

After taking my blood glucose level, I measure out the insulin units and carry out the injection. The injection hurts, and no matter how many times the nurse tells me I will get used to it right now that is not happening. For breakfast, I have two cups of Cheerios, one cup of milk, and a pinch of artificial sweetener. Between breakfast and lunch, I have a small snack that consists of a half cup of apple juice and a slice of cheese. When lunch comes around, I take my blood sugar level again and measure out my insulin. I eat a peanut butter and jelly sandwich, a snack size bag of chips, and one cup of milk. Before dinner starts, I have to take my blood level again for another reading and measure out insulin. Dinner is the only meal that is different. I always look forward to dinner because it isn't the same exact thing every single day. This eating routine continues for a couple of months.

Another change in my routine is waking up every two hours in the middle of the night to check my blood glucose level. Being newly diagnosed with juvenile diabetes requires me to have a set amount of insulin. This set amount of insulin is never easy to figure out so I am put on a trial basis to see what measurements will work the best. Because of this I have to wake up every two hours to see if my blood level is okay throughout the night. The hospital doesn't want to risk my blood level rising too much or dropping too low while I am sleeping.

Nothing feels the same anymore. Ever since this happened everything about my day to day routine of life has been completely altered. Going to bed isn't the same and sleeping is entirely different. Even things like eating are different because of my new food restrictions and the need for me to count out carbohydrates for every piece of food I consume. Most of the time I am in my bedroom as opposed to being at school or going outside to run around for hours on end.

My mother stays in my room most of the nights since returning from the hospital. I feel guilty for her staying there, but it is comforting at the same time. I turn over in my bed to see her sleeping on the floor. To think of all the pain I have caused her, and may continue to cause her, creates a deep feeling of sadness inside of me. I have no idea what it is like to be a parent and see a child go through this. I wish I can go to her, quietly wake her up, and tell her everything is going to be okay. I wish I can tell her the juvenile diabetes is going to go away and all of this will be a thing of the past. But I know I can't. I can't even tell myself that everything is going to be okay.

The pain grows inside of me as I look over at my mother. The emotional pain she is going through isn't fair. The pain is because of me and this new disease I have recently been diagnosed with. I start to cry again. I don't want to wake her up. I know she needs her sleep because she has gotten almost as little as I have lately. So I turn towards the wall and cry in my hands again. Soon enough, my hands and my pillow are covered in tears.

Being diagnosed at the age of twelve is hard. Being diagnosed with a disease or illness at any age is difficult. At the age of twelve I am old enough to be curious about what has happened and want to find answers. I am not young enough to wait for my parents to explain everything or old enough to know what type one diabetes is. I am at the age where I am trapped between waiting for answers and trying to find them on my own.

Diagnosed with diabetes is not the life I should be living. A twelve-year-old should not have to learn how to measure insulin and calculate blood glucose levels. I shouldn't have to count carbohydrates and have a limit to a certain amount of food for every single meal. I should be able to eat a package full of cookies and ruin my dinner like a normal kid does. I want to get yelled at for ruining my dinner. Not because I am diabetic, but because I shouldn't eat cookies before dinner. I should feel dirty because I am going outside and tackling my brother in the dirt while playing football. I should be getting treatment because I have scrapes on my knees and blood on my hands from playing sports and going on adventures with my neighbors. I don't feel this way though. I don't even have enough strength to walk around for a few minutes without feeling dizzy.

I feel dirty because of the calluses on my fingers and syringe tracks on my arms. I feel disgusting because when I seek medical treatment it is for the purpose of taking care of the disease that has taken control of my life. I will not feel any different until this disease is out of my life; and as far as I know this disease has no cure and will be with me forever.

I sit in my bed at night and think about everything going on. Once again, all the questions and mixed feelings are swirling around in my head. Out of control and fast paced. Painful and unbearable. Unimaginable and unwanted. As I sit in my bed, a realization comes to me. A profound and exact recognition that will without a doubt affect the rest of my life.

There is a feeling inside that I have lost control of my life. The juvenile diabetes is now in control and is in the driver's seat. I am helplessly strapped in the passenger seat. I have to follow its rules and travel on its highway, and there is nothing I can do about it. I have to live according to what it does. It tears me up inside to feel that I don't have any control of my life.

I lost something. I lost a part of me. The moment I was diagnosed with juvenile diabetes, a part of me was lost forever. I lost my health. I didn't lose a loved one. I didn't move. I didn't lose a best friend or lose a pet to an early death, but I did lose something. I missed the chance to live a healthy life like all the people around me. I lost my pancreas, the ability to produce insulin in a normal, healthy way and to break down the sugars I ingest. I lost that functioning part of a healthy body, and I can't get it back.

Dealing with this illness is not the most common form of loss, but it is still a loss. I never had the chance to grieve what I lost. Doctors, nurses, family, friends, students, and teachers constantly tell me everything is okay, and I will move on. I can't deny thinking that everything is not okay. I understand everyone's reason for saying this. They don't want me to sit in my pity and become depressed over what has happened. They want to try their hardest to push me forward and move on from what has happened.

But is it really okay? Am I supposed to wake up the next morning in the hospital, learning about juvenile diabetes, and think to myself that it is okay? It is not okay. Okay is the complete opposite. My life is a disaster, and I don't know how to grab a hold of it. When people tell me that everything is okay, and I will bounce back in no time, I feel like I am wrong for feeling the way I do. I have so many feelings associated with what has just happened. I am feeling hate, sadness, anger, frustration, fear, torn, broken, trapped, and lost. I feel all of these things yet everyone tells me it will be alright. So I shut down. I don't tell people how I feel because I don't feel as if it is acceptable. When people tell me it's okay, I simply shake my head and give them the gesture that I agree.

Maybe I need someone to tell me how it is. Maybe I need someone to look me straight into my dark eyes and tell me that what has just happened is far from okay and that I am far from being okay. I need someone to be stronger than me and hold nothing back. I hurt enough as it is so what is the harm in being honest with me? I am very far away from being okay – and I don't know when I will ever be at that point.

CHAPTER 3

Coming Back to Reality

"Life is not a problem to be solved, but a reality to be experienced."

Quote Inspired by Soren Kierkegaard

During the time of my recovery, in the hospital and at home, my mind is lost in this maze and catching up with reality seems nearly impossible. This maze is pitch black. The different paths I can take consists of hundreds of questions going through my mind. Answering the questions will lead me in that particular direction. I think the more questions I answer the closer I will get to find the way out of this maze. If I can answer the question as to what my life is supposed to be like, then I can escape. The problem is the questions have no answers, and I feel forever lost in the dark maze.

I can't come to grips with what has happened. As strange as it seems everything is out of place, and I feel different even in my skin. I barely sleep. The reality of what is happening outside of my head is blocked out, and it just leaves me paralyzed. I try as long as I can but escaping reality forever is impossible. The first reality check comes the night before I return to school. Tonight I don't sleep any more than a few hours. School bag is packed and ready to go, and my clothes are hanging over the chair in my room.

The whole night I continue asking myself a hundred more questions. These questions are relating to my peer relationships and how I imagine being treated at school. The questions never stop coming. *How come my classmates never came to visit me in the hospital? How are they going to treat me now? Am I different from everyone else? Is anyone going to make fun of me for having juvenile diabetes? Do they understand what happened to me? Are girls every going to want to go out with me?* The questions go on and on throughout the night in a vicious, repetitive cycle.

Getting ready for school the next morning creates a nervous wreck inside of me. I have no idea what to expect the first day coming back. Everything feels different from waking up, to getting ready, and being back in school. I am back in a familiar surrounding amongst classmates but at the same time it is an experience that is not comparable to any other times I walked throughout these halls.

The first interaction with my classmates went very well. Some of them ask how I am feeling and others say they are glad to see me back in school. Concentrating in school becomes impossible. The rest of sixth grade and all of seventh grade became an academic battle. How can I think about mathematics and social studies when I have to answer all the other questions in my head? My grades start slipping, and I am averaging C's and D's. Doing poorly in my classes doesn't bother me.

School starts to become a complete blur now while sitting in the classrooms day after day. Even though I am here, it's like my mind is nowhere close to where it should be. I'm off staring into space while the textbooks, pencils, and paper sit there without purpose. I am tired too from continuously waking up in the middle of the night every two hours to check my blood and attempting to go back to sleep again. Sometimes I can't even remember if I fell asleep at all.

Most of my recovery time is spent searching for answers. I don't know any of the answers to the questions. And without having answers, the questions keep coming and coming. The whole mystery becomes a jigsaw puzzle all messed up into a thousand different pieces. I don't know where some of them are, and most of the time I can't even understand what the parts are telling me. Throughout my recovery, I keep searching for clues and pieces to this new life of mine.

I start to search the house to find clues and information regarding what happened to me. Searching to find some hospital report to explain what happened. One day I hear the phone ring, and when I pick it up it is my godfather. He asks to speak to my dad, and I open the basement door and yell down the steps to pick up the phone. Before I hang up the phone, I hear them talk for a couple of seconds.

"How is he doing?" my godfather asks.

"We almost lost him." My father responds.

Right at that moment it felt like time froze. Feet are still and the phone is still next to my ear, but I can't hear anything. Finally, time starts up again; I hang the phone up, and I immediately head to my room and sit down on my bed. Until that point, I never knew I almost died. I had no clue how close I was to dying. I understood everything that happened was a big deal, but until that point I had no idea how severe it truly was. Panic begins to kick in, and the thoughts kept pouring into my head, over and over again. I can't stop thinking about everything. Even when I try, the thoughts kept coming.

I don't know what to think. I don't even know what it means that I almost died. I can't hold back anymore, and I have to let go. I try to stop myself, but the force is overbearing. I put my hands over my eyes, nose, and mouth and cry uncontrollably. Does any of it mean anything?

I keep receiving more puzzle pieces to the mystery. A friend of mine tells me about a conversation his mother had with mine.

"My mom talked to your mom on the phone last night," he says.

"Oh," I respond. "What about?"

"About you. Your mom told my mom that if she hasn't taken you to the hospital in two hours you would have been dead."

"Is that true?" someone asks a few spots down the table.

Everyone's eyes are on me. I have no choice but to respond by saying, "Yeah. Yeah, it is."

I don't eat any more of my lunch after that. Two hours sticks in my head the rest of the day at school and throughout the night. No idea what the means if anything at all. *What if my mom never came home to check up on me? What if she went out for lunch and didn't even think about coming back? What if my condition got worse and I had less than two hours to live?* I couldn't imagine having only two hours left before I would have been dead.

The clues are starting to make sense, but at the same time I don't want to see the final picture. I start talking to my parents about what had happened that day. When you are young, you think your parents have all the answers for you. So when you go to them with questions, you always think they will come up with some answer, even if it's not the truth. This time I will not receive any answers because my parents don't have any. They can't explain to me what the reason is for me acquiring juvenile diabetes. They can't tell me why this has to happen me.

Frequently questioning what is going on starts to become an unhealthy way of trying to figure out what was going on. When I tried to avoid talking about my condition and everything about diabetes I would hope that I could move far past and beyond it. But, when I finally started getting some distance something about it would come up or occur that would bring me back into wanting to figure out why this all happened. It becomes so chaotic, going back and forth between not wanting to know anything about it on one hand to wanting to come face to face with the truth of my diabetes on the other.

I start blaming myself for what happened to me. I feel as if I am an evil person who deserves to have this disease. I feel as if I did something wrong in my life and this is God's way of punishing me. I start to lose my belief and faith in God. So many people ask the question, "Why does God let bad things happen to good people?" I start to ask the same thing and become even more hurt and frustrated when he does not answer. If he can't answer, then what faith do I have that my questions will have any answers?

I try and ask God why this had to happen to me. *Why God? Why did this happen to me?* I can ask the question a hundred times a day, and He continues to avoid responding. He leaves me here in silence without any support or clue. From this point on I start blaming God as well for what has happened to me.

One day the entire truth of that day is explained to me. I don't know how long my parents struggled to find the right time to do this. They most likely fought individually, as a couple, and even as a family to try and explain something they did not truly understand either. I'm sure it drove them to many sleepless nights, constant concern and worry about their son. Not knowing what to say about what happened and most importantly probably scared about what to do now.

My parents sat me down and explained that when I had the flu, in an attempt to fight off the sickness, the antibodies in me attacked the pancreas. There is no known cure for juvenile diabetes, also known as type one diabetes. Having type one diabetes is primarily becoming insulin dependent. I will rely on insulin to live the rest of my life. My mother explained when she took me to the hospital their blood monitor couldn't read the blood glucose level. The hospital transported me over to another hospital by ambulance. The first hospital could only measure blood glucose levels to a maximum of one-thousand. Listening to the nurses and watching educational videos on living with diabetes I learn soon enough that my blood sugar level should be between eighty and one-hundred and twenty.

My mother explains my blood glucose level was around fourteen-hundred. Fourteen-hundred is the level the hospital uses to say, "This person will die." I didn't die, and there is still some purpose for my existence. No one can explain why I have juvenile diabetes. I also found out later there was a chance they almost had to amputate my feet. From what I remember the nurse was trying to get blood and first tried to take blood from my feet. My feet were cold to the point they were numb. They were so purple and cold the nurse was unable to get any blood from them.

Before all this, being a healthy kid was just a part of my daily life. I was active and eating probably better than most other kids my age. Everything about my life before this represented a healthy lifestyle. A healthy childhood up to this point is one of the many reasons to the surprise of my diagnosis. The doctors explain I was probably experiencing some early signs of diabetes as early as December that went unnoticed due to the amount of physical activity I was getting on a regular basis. I was diagnosed in April, so that leaves less than four months where I was going through the transition of becoming insulin dependent.

How could this be though? How could I play in basketball games on the weekends and practice if I were having health problems? Why weren't my teachers able to notice weird behaviors and odd symptoms? How come my physician couldn't see anything during my physical exams and other appointments? How did this disease escape past everyone and come crashing into my life?

I thought finding all these answers would be the solution to everything. Maybe if they told me everything I could figure out what to do about what life was going to be like from here on out. The only problem is that everything I hear leads to more frustration, anger, hurt, and depression. Everything I learn only helps the hatred grow inside of me. Hate the condition itself and everything it has caused.

The irrational thoughts about having juvenile diabetes start to become rational in my mind. At first, it is the compulsive, rapid thoughts that are going on in my head. I don't verify them or deny them either, but acknowledged their presence. Life feels far from normal. Trying to balance school, peers, family, the doctors, trying to find answers, and managing diabetes becomes a task I cannot even begin to understand fully. My mind wanders off in a hundred different directions and then all of the sudden comes crashing back down to reality.

Maybe if things could just begin to feel normal again, I could make it through the hardship. But, that becomes a struggle when individual peers at school start cracking jokes about my diabetes. Some peers call me names like dirty diabetic, diabetic donut, and diabetes boy. They make sarcastic remarks about sugar, injections, syringes, and other associations with my diabetes.

The jokes went on for a long time. To some peers, it feels as if I am not even the same I was before all of this happened. Maybe they are right. Instead, I am known simply as the diabetic. Being ridiculed and embarrassed by my peers due to my disease is the start of my dark depression because instead of thinking I can come back to how things were I see now that this is my reality. I start to hate life and everything else that has resulted after that day. No longer do I feel as if I belong among others. I hate my diabetes and what it causes me. I come home from school with the emotional pain stirring around inside of me. I feel different. I feel dirty. I feel disgusting. I feel like I am all alone, and nobody wants to be associated with a diabetic.

The worst part of it all is that I cannot escape from the diabetes. I can leave school and not be there when some students are making fun of me. I can leave the hospital and staff when they are trying to treat me. I can even avoid my parents when I don't want to deal with something regarding school or diabetes. But one thing is for sure, my reality has changed to wherever I go diabetes is constantly there.

There are times when I attempt to go back and feel like things can be exactly the way they were before. A good friend calls and invites me to a party he is going to have at his parent's house over the weekend. It was something to look forward to outside of what was going on. A party with classmates is a relieving sign I am still a part of ordinary adolescent living.

Feeling different from everyone else comes into my head at a party that became another reality check. I head over to a friend's house, and as I arrive at the party and walk through the familiar kitchen I notice platters and bowls of snack food for everyone. I ate dinner right before I left to go to his house. There is pizza, snack mixes, and beverages sprawled out all over their kitchen counter. Before I had diabetes, I wouldn't hesitate at all to thank his parents and indulge in normal teenage snacking.

It's different now though. I am not allowed to have any food anytime I want. I have to wait until later at night when I go home. By that time, I will be in bed, no one will be around, and the food will be all gone. I can't even eat a simple piece of food anymore at a party. When friends ask if I want anything or if they can get me anything I have to deny them and say I can't. Something as simple as eating food becomes a different reality and way of living.

Realizing I can't eat food whenever I want to, or join in with my friends to grab a slice of pizza or a handful of trail mix, creates anxiety and an overwhelming sense of being uncomfortable. Deep down I feel I am not like everyone else. It feels as if I am different and I can't live a normal life like the rest of my peers. The rest of my stay at the party is spent sitting on a couch, going through the hundreds of questions I am asking myself.

The discomfort, anxiety, and complete sense of confusion continues to build. I begin to be in a depressed mood most of the day. I have diminished interest in almost all activities most of the day. I quit drawing because I feel like it will never become to anything because of having diabetes. During the initial stay in the hospital after my diagnosis, I remember family members coming to visit. My two aunts come to visit and bring a pad of sketch paper and drawing pencils to keep me occupied. I remember sitting there and trying to think of something, anything to put on paper.

Drawing is one of my greatest joys. Since a young childhood, and seeing my first few Disney movies, I dreamed of becoming an artist and bringing characters to life through pages of art. I would draw cartoons all day long and in all my school notebooks. Pictures would go to family and friends without hesitating. It was the inspiration, creativity, and imagination that took the ideas in my head and able to transform them on paper. I sat there, in that hospital bed, not being able to draw a single thing. Now the sketch pad sits in my room with nothing but empty pages.

I spend a lot of time being isolated from everyone, asking myself more questions and having no sense at all about what to do. Hours turn into days. Days turn into weeks. Weeks turn into months. It all adds up where days start to lose meaning. There is nothing to look forward to and nothing on the horizon but more finger pokes, insulin injections, carb counting, and visits to the hospital. Living like this has gone on for over a year and a half, and the thoughts and feelings inside lead to heavier questions regarding the future. I start to contemplate the question, *is it worth being alive?* The tunnel of my life becomes darker and darker. I don't know what is going to happen in my life, and I am desperately attempting to grab a hold of any light that I can.

Reaching the Top Before
Hitting the Bottom

*"Some of us can be examples about going
ahead and growing, and some of us,
unfortunately, don't make it there."*

Quote Inspired by Stevie Ray Vaughan

Eighth grade brought about changes in life that I did not see ever coming true since the diagnosis. It was unexpected, simple and yet gave an opportunity for the light to shine back in and find a way out of this misery. My health is at a stable condition, and it's at a point where I am comfortable going through the regular maintenance. I struggle with seeing anything else in life, but diabetes and it's daily requirements are becoming somewhat of a miserable way of living. At least all of the finger pokes and insulin injections continue to blur together.

I'm still waiting for the doctors to call me and say there is a cure. If they could just find a cure I would do anything they ask of me. I would take care of my health and do everything they needed as long as they can cure this illness. But a cure still isn't found. I have the misconceptions I can't do anything, have no meaning, am different from everyone else, and live with such uncertainty. I did find something though that had a powerful impact on how I viewed myself and the condition of my health. A lot of the misconceptions swirling inside my head about being diabetic started to change because of this newfound opportunity.

Confidence is lacking; however I decide to go out on a limb and try out for the basketball team in eighth grade. Days before tryouts I keep recalling the good moments and times I had played before all of this happened. The teams are divided up between the A team and B team. The A team players are selected for more talent to play against the other teams with an equal level of skill. Surprisingly, I didn't think about trying to make the team, and doubts and concerns were entirely absent. Being on the court, holding the basketball, and taking a long distance shot takes me away from everything going on. It is comforting being here and just doing what I normally did as a child growing up.

After tryouts, I am shocked and almost stunned to discover that not only did I make the team, but I was good enough to make the A team for my school. I didn't even know what to say at first. And nothing was said at all. The idea that I am not going to be able to accomplish anything changes. I overcome the misconception and prove I could play sports, even at a high level. Everything changes. And by everything, I mean, nearly everything about what had just happened over the past year and half seems to be wiped clean.

Since the start of my first practice, till my last game on the court, basketball creates a different environment around me and an entirely different world inside of me. I am nervous coming to the first practice. I know the other players and some of them are already top athletes. A talented soccer player, a point guard with good ball handling skills, a tall figure who towers over everyone, a sharp shooter with a competitive push, and then there's me. I have no idea what I was going to bring to this team or how this was going to play out. But, I know that playing basketball is like stepping out of my skin and being someone else. And being the basketball player is a hell of a lot better than being the diabetic.

I am always nervous before every single basketball game. I always come to the games early to sit in the bleachers and take in the whole atmosphere of the gym. During the first couple of games I am quiet and conservative. Being on the basketball is full of such peace and tranquility that diabetes took away from me. The game almost gives me a chance to slow down and not worry about all the other uncertainties in life.

I become known for my outside shooting, and that's what I bring to the table. The practice and games with teammates. Playing in the driveway with my brother and neighborhood friends. Talking to my parents about basketball. Being seen as one of the basketball players at school. I may not be the best basketball player, but it is hard to imagine finding someone else who feels how important basketball is to them. Thinking about upcoming practices, teams we are going to play, wondering which fellow students are going to show up, and how many three-pointers I am going to make floods my mind. Most importantly, it pushes all of the doubts, concerns, and miseries related to diabetes out.

A little commotion at school starts to rise about the amount of three pointers me and the sharpshooter could make all season. Some of the students at school and basketball teammates start keeping track of how many three-pointers we make throughout the season. Walking in the hallways other students wish me luck in games and ask me how many three-pointers I am going to make. I no longer worry if they are thinking of my diabetes. I don't shy away from conversation or stare off into space contemplating what's going to happen next with my health or my life. I feel normal again among teammates and classmates.

All I care about is basketball. Basketball and my teammates. Rapport with my teammates starts growing at a faster pace. I talk to them more during classes and even outside of school. I spend time with the guys at school and on the weekends we play basketball. Not only am I known as a basketball player now, but I feel like I finally belong somewhere in a group of friends. Ever since the diagnosis of diabetes I was searching for a place to belong. I felt all alone in a world that no one understood. With basketball and my teammates, I feel as if I belong among them.

With basketball in my life it takes the place of my diabetes. No longer do I have the compulsive, fast thoughts in my head about finger pokes, injections, insulin, appointments, or doctors. Now all the habitual, rapid thoughts in my head are all about basketball. *Are we going to win this weekend? Who are we playing? Am I going to play well? How many three-pointers are the sharp shooter and I going to make? Who's going to come to the game and watch?*

Basketball was not only a way to have a sense of belonging but it was a healthy activity. Part of my treatment of diabetes is to exercise and be active. At first, I was very lazy and unmotivated to do any physical activity. Most of the time I wanted to stay in bed and stay isolated from the world. Playing basketball became a motivational force to stay healthy and provided a reason to actually care about diabetes.

I start to adapt the basketball strategies with other areas in my life. My confidence grows stronger and stronger. Another misconception quickly changes in my life. A month or so into the basketball season and I have my first girlfriend. One of the misconceptions I had returning to school was that girls would not want to go out with me because of the diabetes. I had thoughts about girls being afraid of diabetes and not wanting to get involved with someone who has it.

Finally, I am back to living the ordinary life of an adolescent. This is everything I have been waiting for since being released from the hospital. School, friends, family, basketball, girls, and weekends are once again in my life. I am looking forward to things once again and have reason to enjoy every day that I can. Life becomes one big basketball game. I start to take everything in life as I do with a three-point shot in basketball. I always feel if I plant my feet right, have the correct grip on the ball, and have a smooth stroke I will have a greater chance of making the shot. I start feeling the same way with everything else. I feel if I can approach someone, simply spark a conversation, and make small talk, then I can make friends. With my confidence increasingly getting stronger I start to make new friends and build more relationships.

I feel like I have found a place of belonging with my group of friends. Life seems different now. Taking care of diabetes becomes a quick task to get it over with so I can move on to other things that are more important. It's not enjoyable. It still hurts when it comes to injections and finger pokes. But I do it because that means staying healthy for basketball. And I need to stay healthy for basketball because it was the spark that had given me a new role in my life. No longer am I the diabetic dealing with health problems. Now I have the role as a friend, boyfriend, and basketball player.

The end of the basketball season is the greatest time for the game. The regular season is over and we are facing a number of upcoming tournaments. The first tournament begins, and we aren't expected to get very far. On the other side of the bracket is the team that is supposed to win hands down. We played them twice and lost to them by double digits in both games. Teams are crumbling to them throughout the tournament. Go figure; this is the team we have to play in the championship match. To imagine us being nervous was an understatement with all the teams already destroying one another.

Everyone came to watch the game. Other players from teams who were already eliminated came and sat in the stands. My family comes to see me play as well as my friends. Before the game starts, I can see friends move their way into the bleachers. I see my girlfriend in the stands with some of her peers. This game is unforgettable as we fought minute to minute with the team that was supposed to wipe us off the floor. In a way though, playing basketball with my teammates was about the sport and it wasn't at the same time. Sometimes being out there wasn't all about basketball but about being out there with amongst people we cared for deeply.

The final buzzer sounds, and we lose the game by three points. It comes down to a last minute shot for us to tie the game, but the attempt comes up short. After the game I go the locker room, listen to the coach's speech, get dressed, and head on out. On my way to greet my friends, and thank them for coming, the director of the tournament comes over to talk to me and another teammate. We are asked to play in the All-Star Game that is to take place in a few weeks. I am shocked to get the invitation. As soon as I walk back my family and friends are all excited to see me. They congratulate me for a tournament well played and for being accepted into the All-Star game.

Playing in the All-Star Game is an incredible moment that makes describing its real impact difficult to do. My family and friends hold up to their statements and come all out for the game. People are wearing shirts with my name, school, number and made signs cheering me on. As my name is announced during the introduction, they all yell and scream at the top of their lungs. When I went to shake my coach's hand he whispered to me, "We know who won the popularity contest." The game went great, as I did my part hitting three baskets from beyond the arc and a couple other shots.

I can't deny that enjoying the popularity was great. While that was awesome having others watch and take notice, the eyes that meant the most were of my family and friends. The ones who believed in me. The ones who supported me. The ones who decided that out of everything they could do with their free time on the weekend they chose to watch me play basketball. They don't do it because they pity me, or worry about me, or was on eggshells of what was going to happen. That's the attention diabetes brought, but basketball brings about everything good about wanting to see a future where success and myself could be one of the same.

My family saw the happiness flourish whenever I played basketball, and that's all they ever wanted. Instead of the constant thoughts of worrying about me, purchasing expensive medical supplies, and working with nurses, they now have other responsibilities when it comes to their son. I gave them the responsibility to come cheer for their child. It is a responsibility I am proud to give them. Watching children playing sports and cheering them on is something a parent should look forward to with eager and pride. I am not the only one living a normal life again, but my parents and siblings are as well. Now, we have other things to talk about besides the condition of my health.

During the initial diagnosis and the time spent in recovery, I was scared for my sister and brother. Both of them didn't come to the hospital. I know what happened that day not only changed my life and my parents, but of my siblings as well. What kind of brother was I being when I had to spend so much time dealing with the diabetes, struggles with school, isolating myself, and not wanting to be around. I see basketball as the opportunity to show them how their brother isn't just a diabetic and I can somehow start to be that person they can admire.

The next big tournament is the greatest stage for grade school basketball. The final competition of the tournament is the March Madness, NBA Playoffs, Stanley Cup, World Series of baseball, and Super Bowl for grade school basketball. Teams from all over are in the tournament with their seeds picked out. Either you win it all and capture the title or your season ends with a loss.

Friends at school help out by decorating our lockers and coming to the games. The atmosphere before the tip-off is insane. Fans are going ballistic before each and every game. Most of them come wearing our team colors of white and green. Many of them make signs and t-shirts. Once again, we are one of the underdogs but after our showing in the first tournament other teams are more aware of us.

We are knocked out in the third round, right before the final four, to the team that eventually wins the entire tournament. After the game all of our fans, including family and friends, are waiting outside the locker room. Even though we lost, and the basketball season is over now, I am not disappointed. I go home, still being happy and content with what has happened even after being handed a defeat. Like I said… in a way it was all about playing basketball and in the end it was not all about basketball.

The season is over, and everything is back to the usual routine of going to classes and spending time with friends on the weekend. Relationships with girls start and break up. Some were more disappointing than others, but in a way it felt like a regular part of life.

The summer goes by real fast. The time is spent having people over, playing basketball in the driveway, and enjoying life. I still have my connections with old basketball teammates. All the time I used to spend isolating in my room is now entirely obsolete. If I wasn't in the driveway playing basketball, I was talking or hanging out with friends. I was taking care of my health because I finally had a reason to care about the future I began to build. If taking care of my diabetes meant being able to be physically well for basketball than that is definitely worth it. If taking care of my diabetes means being able to see friends than I was willing to do that.

It finally hits me that high school is right around the corner. The decision on which high school to attend is not too concerning. Going from grade school to high school, the decision is primarily set by where friends are going. I really have no clue what the deciding factor is going be. It comes down to the fact that my older sister and older cousin already attend high school together and then I find out my cousin who is the same age is going to the school they attend. With family members going to the same school, I figure it is in my best interest to go there. I didn't put much thought into it and why should I?

The truth of the matter is life right now is better than I could ever imagine. The insecurities of diabetes are not in my mind anymore. The condition of my physical health is exceptional because I want to take care of it. As long as I have basketball I will have my answer to overcoming all the struggles I dealt with in the past. Basketball has become the magic answer that I searched so desperately to find ever since being diagnosed. But, now I have been able to find a reason to take care of it, and basketball has given me that answer to the question I asked for quite some time.

Starting to Get Slippery

"The greatest accomplishment is not in never falling, but in rising again after you fall."

Quote Inspired by Vince Lombardi

This high school appears to be an acceptable place to attend. The building isn't falling apart or anything, so I imagine it is going to work out just fine. As soon as I walk into school I was immediately looking for familiar faces. I still have the strong connection with the basketball players. The tall guy lives behind the house across the street and his sister conveniently starts taking us to school every day. The sharpshooter and I immediately begin talking about the upcoming basketball season and the chance to represent the school. I notice the soccer player down a few lockers from me and everything appear to be settling in well.

I meet some new people and begin to establish some friendships with them. The reality of high school hit pretty quickly when I start to realize the number of students there outweighed what I was used to back in grade school. There was a point I was finally beginning to feel more comfortable among my fellow peers and have a sense of belonging among the entire class. High school was entirely different.

It was only a few people that I knew and instead of having classes with everyone it became having a few or even none at all.

The familiar idea of feeling like a fish out of water begins to sink in. When I am around my friends and basketball players it is comforting; but when they are not around I begin to isolate again and stay quiet. It did not take long for my diabetes to suffer from these insecurities. I would start to feel embarrassed at the thought of excusing myself from class to go and take an insulin injection before lunch. Peers in grade school would know I was leaving to take my insulin and would look forward to seeing me at lunch. But these new people do not know about my diabetes, and that's the way I would prefer it.

Instead of having the courage and strength to take care of my diabetes I decided to take the other route and hide it and keep it a secret. I carried my insulin and syringes around in a brown paper bag rolled up. Most of the time I would forget to bring my blood meter and even when it was there I avoided taking it. There were times I excused myself to go to the bathroom, close the stall door, draw up the insulin and inject it right there.

I feel like I'm hiding something and doing something wrong and shameful. The idea of doing it over and over again, day after day, begins to develop this dirty feeling that each and every time drove me further to wanting to simply not do it again. I despised it each and every time. At the very moment, or thought, that someone would question why I was constantly going to the bathroom the same time during class created more insecurities. If I ever felt someone was getting the faintest concern or wonder, I would avoid going. And that meant completely forgetting to take my insulin.

Classes, teachers, and fellow students start to become that similar blur again. Concentrating in school became difficult once again just like after returning home from the hospital. I could tell I was beginning to lose interest again. The focus wasn't there, and the questions automatically circulate in and out of my mind again like ones before. The weekends aren't helpful either. I never spend time with anyone from this school. Everyone seems busy doing other things and going to parties and building new friendships.

During the first couple of months I sit at home and work for my father's business in the basement. It becomes a place of escape for me to leave school and find my way downstairs to work side by side with my dad. There are a lot of things I want to tell him and talk about but can't muster up the courage to do so. At least sitting down here and working for him is comforting just having him at the desk next to me.

Basketball tryouts are coming up and this is the first time I feel excited at school. Life here at school for the first couple months is getting to be lonely and uneventful. Basketball can easily change all of that. Floods of positive memories from the basketball days brings relief. If I make the basketball team, I can find my place of belonging once again. I can find acceptance among my fellow peers and the potential to make friends will be overwhelming.

I am anticipating tryouts to be successful. I know some of the players from teams in grade school, and I feel I can compete with them. My over enthusiastic viewpoint proves to be an overwhelming disappointment. At the end of the day they post the names of people who are to come back the next day for the second part of tryouts. Out of the four of us from the grade school team, I am the only one not selected. I don't say anything after we get picked up and drive home. One of the guys comes back to my house and I'm completely silent. He can tell I am not taking the news well, and I don't say bye as he walks out the door. In the end, another player would be cut after the second day, and the soccer player and sharpshooter made the freshman team.

Not making the basketball team is a devastating crush on me. That feeling of reality sinking in was more of a crash this time. I know beforehand if I don't make the team it would hurt. I am at a new school, with students whom I am not friends with, searching for a role to fit in and belong. In grade school, basketball proved to do that. Being on the basketball team meant the entire world to me. It made everything that happened to me in the past go away for the moment or be on the sidelines.

It helped me take care of the diabetes because I wanted to be healthier. Being cut from the team takes all of that away. Confidence to make new friends and be social goes from low to completely absent. I have no confidence whatsoever to strike a conversation with someone or to try and make friends. After all, when friends ask you that day if you made the team, and you say no, it is not the best feeling in the world. I even begin to avoid my old friends from grade school and view them like everyone else.

My life feels empty without basketball. Feelings inside of me create doubt, shame, and failure. I don't have many friends, I don't have a girlfriend, basketball is now out of the picture, and my happiness and healthy way of living is starting to slip. After I find out basketball isn't going to be a part of my life the condition of my diabetes begins to fade. Everything went from being great and enjoying my life to re-living the hate experienced before.

Basketball was the missing piece in the puzzle that served as a healthy substitute for neglecting my health. Not only is it a benefit towards my physical health, but it changed the feelings inside by feeling a place of belonging and acceptance. After it is gone the closest way to cope was going back to old ways and past behaviors. Some of the former teammates and friends try and keep my spirits up.

With everyone else though, I begin to fit in my old role again. I begin to think more about the meaning in my life, and why I'm still here after diabetes should have killed me. I hate my life once again for what it has done. I begin to see myself even more different from everyone at school because of it. I feel different and alone. I feel dirty. I feel disgusting. And I feel like I don't belong here at all.

The signs of my depression start creeping back into my life. Instead of trying to fight it and find reasons for happiness I let the pain come back to me. I never take care of my health anymore. My diabetes is getting worse and worse by the day. I am not taking my insulin all the time, rarely taking my blood, and never care about what I am eating. Even when I do manage to sneak away to the nearest bathroom stall and unroll the paper bag with the syringe and insulin, I anticipate something to happen. Anyone else coming into the bathroom or feeling like it was taking too much time gave me a reason to stop and avoid giving myself the insulin.

The compulsive, fast paced questions are pouring through my mind. Every day and every night the questions come in and out of my head; creating frustration, stress, anger, depression, and feelings of hatred towards my life. For a long time, I broke free from the chains of pain that diabetes caused. I was happy with my life, with friends, with basketball, and having a girlfriend. And within a couple of months everything is turned upside down.

My relationships with some of the people I met at school slowly diminish and I reach out to old friends who attend a high school closer to home. During a random day, I stare off into space at school as usual and think about how great everything was in grade school. Everything and everyone around me are in a far distant are and I could care less. So far, it hasn't done anything for me, and these people could care less. It's disappointing when my mind wonders back to reality, and I'm sitting in a classroom in a school with peers who feel like complete strangers. I stay up late tonight and can't seem to go to bed. I ask myself a thousand questions and wish for anything that I could be on the basketball team.

Minutes turn into hours, and I can't keep myself up anymore. I lie down and hope that some magical source of the powers that be will change everything back to the way it was. My eyes get heavy, and before I know it I am sleeping. All of the sudden I wake up and I am lying down in an ambulance, looking through the windows. Through the small window, I can see the sitting on top of the hill. My head is spinning and my vision turns pitch black.

As I wake up, I feel nurses and doctors surrounding me. They are poking and touching me all over my body trying to apply care. All of the nurses are describing what they are doing to me. One is telling me about the intravenous lines going through my arms. Another is explaining how much insulin is being pumped throughout my body. One nurse at the end of the bed is trying to poke my feet, but I cannot feel a thing. I want to be left alone. I feel weird. I feel disgusting. I want them to go.

All of the sudden I awake from my sleep. I am sweating and my heart is racing. I am in my bed at home, and I realize I was having another nightmare. I don't want to go back to bed. I don't want the nightmare to enter my mind again, so I resist getting any sleep. I get up and go over to my desk. I pop in a movie and begin doing work for my father's company. I work all night until the next morning when I have to go to school.

The nightmares start coming back and it creates a feeling of complete dread. One of the scariest feelings is never knowing what your mind is going to do when you fall asleep, and now that the nightmares start coming back I fear the next time one will come. It was months since I had a nightmare prior to this. I still didn't sleep as much but that was because of the excitement of a basketball game the next day, or seeing some friends at school, or looking forward to what was going to happen. Sleepless nights are once again caused by all the concern, fear, worry, and doubt.

Even though I continue to slip, I haven't fallen yet. I believe I can recoup during the summer when I don't have to be reminded every day of being in school where I feel like I don't belong. For the most part, I spend with old friends from grade school and working for my father's company hours on end. Working for him is the only thing I am good at doing and at least was a way I could make up for not making the basketball team and being a disappointment. The basement becomes my safe haven.

The sophomore year comes around sooner than I expect. Nothing changes at all from the point I walked out the doors for summer break. What should I expect when I did not do anything different? My friendships with everyone resume in the same place they were before. Some relationships even become nonexistent. Grades are getting even worse. Average grades are mostly D's and even F's. Everything at school is crumbling to the ground. I lost real friendships now and didn't even talk to some of the old basketball teammates.

The communication between particular friends and I are severed. It went from talking every day in school, to a couple times a week, to one day a week, and then nothing. The communication is slipping away, and I don't do anything to stop it from occurring. The rejection, lack of self-confidence, sense of being different and awkwardness prevents me from seeking out ways to fix the broken connections. I could have done different things such as calling, talking more in the hallways, and making the effort to stay in contact. Anything to keep the connection with the people whom I could talk to and trust should have been worth doing.

I finally fall after everything appears to be going wrong. My depression is at its all-time high. Nothing is going right for me anymore. I become so depressed that I start doing something that I can't believe I did. I am taking four insulin injections per day. I am taking one dose for breakfast, one for lunch, one for dinner, and one at night that will last the following day. The insulin injections during the day are to break down the carbohydrates and sugar that I eat at meals.

When everything starts to go bad, I stop taking care of my diabetes and my overall health entirely. Before it was a few times, and then it went to happening more often. Now, I rarely take my blood glucose level during the beginning of my sophomore year. I never know what it is half the time, and I don't care. I don't want to live my life as a diabetic anymore, and I start to ignore the constant reminders of being diabetic. I feel so out of place already, and the last thing I want to do is tell people that I have diabetes.

I don't even know if the school knows I am diabetic. I am never asked to come to the health room and take my insulin before I eat. When I returned to school back in grade school, it was a lot different. My parents met with the teachers, school officials, and nursing staff. All the teachers were made aware of what happened, and I was given permission to leave class before lunch and have everything taken care of for my diabetes. As much as I hated the attention I received, it was a good feeling knowing that I didn't have to deal with this on my own.

I am back to feeling alone on this as I keep it a secret from people at school. I feel disgusting. I feel dirty. I feel ashamed. I am alone when I take my medicine and have no one to be by my side. It hurts every time I decide to inject the syringe into my arm. I am alone when I inflict pain upon myself that doctors tell me I have to do the rest of my life. Most of all, I am angry that I have to do this. I am angry that I have to live this way. Living a secret life that carries an incredible amount of shame. Living a life that I don't want to live.

Having to hide something, and keep the secret of who I am, becomes a routine part of my life. I don't think others will understand or will even want to know. Hiding, lying, keeping secrets, and neglecting to tell the truth starts to become a habit. Every day at school I go to lunch, eat an excessive amount of carbohydrates, and not take my insulin. My lunch consists of five exchanges. One exchange equals fifteen grams of carbohydrates. During lunch, I am allowed to eat seventy-five grams of carbohydrates. For every exchange I eat, this requires two units of insulin to inject. To sum all of it up, I eat seventy-five carbohydrates and measure ten units of insulin to inject. Not only do I stop taking my insulin, I start eating more carbohydrates.

My lunch consists of a cinnamon crunch bagel (75 grams of carbohydrates), one iced tea (34g), and a pretzel (36g). In total that equals 145g of carbohydrates. This brakes down to roughly ten exchanges for me, twice as much as I usually eat. I should be taking twenty units of insulin for this amount of food I am consuming. Most of the time I don't take any insulin, and again, I don't care.

I continue this pattern for an extended period. I continue to avoid taking my insulin, disregarding the duty of counting my carbohydrates, and refusing to take my blood glucose level. Many people think of all the pain and physical symptoms I am going through. It's true; I am going through symptoms of having high blood levels. I am often urinating and have a constant thirst. It is hard for me to concentrate, and I become irritated. My demeanor is that of a sluggish and exhausted person as fatigue is constantly happening.

However, not taking my blood and not taking my insulin does something I have been searching for since I was ever diagnosed with diabetes; *feeling normal again.* By not taking my insulin and not doing everything a diabetic should be doing I don't feel like a diabetic anymore. I feel normal by going to lunch and eating whatever I want to and not having to worry. I feel a personal relief through the pain of not taking care of myself.

For a long time, I feel trapped in this prison of my mind and body fighting against diabetes. This is my escape. This is my way out of the maze of compulsive thinking and irrational thoughts. I am free from the burden of living as a diabetic. I am normal again, and even though it is painful, it provides a certain sense of comfort. I don't see myself as a diabetic anymore. I am aware that if I continue to do this I will more than likely die as a result of not taking care of my diabetes. I am conscious of the fact but it doesn't matter. I tell myself even if I do die because I am not taking care of myself at least I won't die feeling like a diabetic.

Neglecting my health makes me feel normal. By avoiding finger pokes, I no longer have the calluses marked all over my fingertips. Avoiding insulin injections prevents needle marks from being tracked all over my arms. The physical pain of every prick and every injection is gone because I don't do it. I avoid having to inflict pain on myself.

I go to doctor's appointments and lie. I lie about my health. I keep everything a secret about the thoughts and feelings about my diabetes. The doctors never ask about any of the emotional issues related to struggling with diabetes. Every appointment I have there is a new doctor working on me. Every time the new doctor walks in they say hello while looking at their papers, reads my chart and carries out the usual routine. And every time I come back it is a new doctor.

With a different doctor coming through the doors, I have no motivation to cooperate. I tell them I forgot my blood glucose meter at home. This prevents them from downloading the numbers. I forge my blood glucose levels in the daily log. By the looks of it my numbers are fantastic. But it is all a lie. I want to walk in there and get out as soon as possible. The health care providers are meaningless to me unless they can provide a cure. They never provide good news or solutions, and it is a constant repetition of telling me to take care of my diabetes.

I am confident the doctors and hospital staff are aware of the fact I am neglecting to look after my health. This is the only viewpoint they see though; me not taking care of my diabetic needs. This is the tip of the iceberg. Neglecting to take care of my diabetic needs is only what the doctors and hospital staff can see above the water. Below the water level is where most of the iceberg is hiding. Through their eyes, I am simply a patient not taking care of myself when deep down below there is a whole different world they forget to understand.

Most of the actual reasons behind my behaviors, thoughts, feelings, and actions are unknown to everyone. They can only see the tip, which describes the neglecting actions I take to damage my health. The unknown part of the iceberg is where the truth is hidden and most of the time individuals don't spend the time to search for the truth hidden beneath the water.

Not taking care of my diabetes is positive for me. Most of the other students at school are unaware of my health condition. People don't know I have type one diabetes or that I am supposed to be taking insulin right before I eat lunch. All I ever wanted was for people to treat me normal and not look at me and think about my health condition.

Without taking my insulin and worrying about my diabetes, I feel others see me in a normal way. I don't think other students see me as a diabetic but as a regular student. Even though it is dangerous and unhealthy for me to avoid taking care of my diabetes, it feels good inside for me not to. Inside the compulsive questions keep going around and around inside my head. *Why should I stop neglecting my health when it feels comforting?*

CHAPTER 6

Dark Days Even When the Sun Is Out

"I have become my own version of an optimist. If I can't make it through one door, I'll go through another door — or I'll make a door. Something terrific will come no matter how dark the present."

Quote Inspired by Rabindranath Tagore

A loud noise comes from outside, and it is the sound of a thunderstorm. Lighting brightens up the sky and lights up my room. I can hear the rain on the rooftop. I sit up and make my way towards the window. I sit at the end of the bed, open the window and stare at the thunderstorm outside. I enjoy looking outside into the darkness. The thunder continues to tear up the sky; the rain is covering the ground and the lightning flashes into the night. The thunderstorm is pleasant to see. Nothing outside is safe from the wetness of the rain, the brightness of the lightning, and the noise of the thunder. I sit here the rest of the night enjoying the thunderstorm. I don't want to go to sleep because I don't wish to experience another nightmare.

My academic performance continues down its mudslide, getting lower and lower. Failing tests and having incomplete homework assignments don't mean anything to me. The same attitude applies to my health. Receiving an F on a test is similar to taking my blood, whenever I do, and seeing the level is over three-hundred. It is easier to not try in school and fail, same as it is easier for me to not take care of myself and expect my health to suffer. Either way, failing a test or having a high blood level doesn't have any effect on me because I am expecting the worse to happen.

Driving to and from school is one of the only things that brings me a sense of enjoyment. It becomes my source of relaxation and relief. Sometimes I feel like picking up my friends, avoiding the usual route to school, and drive across the country. But, reality always sits in as we make our way to school day after day. It's strange that I never start skipping school. For some reason I feel that would bring more attention; so instead of skipping I sit there in misery.

During the beginning of the year one of the old basketball teammates, who goes to a different school, introduces me to an acquaintance of his. After a couple of dates and conversations I start dating his friend. If it weren't for her confidence and initiation, it wouldn't have happened at all. I was respectful, but for the most part I was still dealing with so many insecurities the thought of a relationship seemed unlikely. But, for whatever reason she felt it was worth pursuing, and we ended up together. She goes to a different high school than I do, but some of my grade school friends happen to attend the same one she does.

Going out with her is another missing piece in the puzzle that I continue to search for at this point. I lost all of my past relationships with girls, and my social life is a disaster. Being with her helps me forget about all the negative aspects of school and the painful struggles I am going through with my diabetes. It doesn't bother me anymore that people at school don't want to hang out. She becomes the source of motivation to go to school every day and get out of class as soon as possible.

My grades continue to slip, but my health begins to make small improvements. I want my health to improve so my relationship with my girlfriend will not be negatively affected by it. It is easy for me to hide the truth about my diabetes from people. I lie to doctors about blood levels and forget to bring my meter for them to download. I tell me parents my blood levels are fine and everything is going great. But everything, deep down inside, is still a mess. I am nowhere near finding a peaceful existence with my diabetes. However, I don't want to lie about it to her so I at least open the door for her to be a part of what I am dealing with. So I take my blood and measure the right amounts of insulin, and I tell her the truth. I find a source of comfort when I am with her.

Everything appears to be getting back on track. Inside I feel deep down that my life is going to be okay and work out as long as I have the motivation to take care of myself. I have fun being with her and enjoy the time we spend together. As I spend time with her, the compulsive thinking about everything begins to go slowly away. It ceases to exist when her presence is near. The horrible existence of my world stops spinning and everything slows down.

It is a typical day, and I go to school wanting to get out immediately and go over to see her. School is routine as always, and the only thing distracting me from the people at school is her. After school, everything becomes a disaster. She breaks up with me shortly after our relationship begins to get serious. For some reason, this breakup is harder than the rest. It is different being with her, and when I lose her it adds to the mix of everything else going wrong.

Instead of having the relationship just end it turns into something worse. Our relationship continues but develops into an arguing and negative display of emotions towards one another. I desperately want this relationship to get better and go back to how it was. What happened? Was it something I did? Even though she wouldn't tell me

I starting getting the idea the persona that everything was okay was really not. I opened a lot of doors and let her into the frustrations at school and health issues.

One of the sources of help I thought could help me get through anything is gone. Now I lost my girlfriend, grades are slipping, and school continues to be a week of misery. It's not surprisingly that my health once again falls off. I go to another doctor's appointment and do the same routine again. It becomes easier to lie, and hide, and manipulate, and escape, and avoid. I felt like she was a part of my life that was going to make a difference. Just like basketball and relationships did back then in the past. But, the past is such a distant memory that it only brings about a pain realizing it is no longer here.

Every day was beginning to feel dreadful. No matter how nice out it seemed, or how enjoyable the time with some friends was, everything at one point became a struggle to make it through the end of the day. I look forward to nothing and whenever something good would come across it became so easy for me to dismiss it quickly.

School is miserable. Grades are awful. Friendships are diminished. Basketball is out of the picture entirely. Health continues to be a constant struggle and pain. And now, the girlfriend and relationship with her is over. Nothing to look forward to and the only thing I have consistently with me all the time is this nightmare of a chronic health condition that has brought my nothing positive in life. It has only left me constantly questioning everything going on and wondering if it has something to do with all the misery in my life.

CHAPTER 7

A Different Scene Could Be the Answer

"The wise man doesn't give the right answers, he poses the right questions."

Quote Inspired by Claude Levi-Strauss

"Another typical school day," a friend says as he pours his cup of coffee.

"I'm sick of these typical days," I respond, with a little anger in my voice. I look at Panera Bread's coffee selection and pick the usual hazelnut.

"What's wrong man?" He asks.

"This is not working for me. I'm not happy here." I add in a little half and half to the coffee.

"Give it time. You'll get used to it." He responds as he adds three sugar packets to his coffee. I can't even have real sugar. I have to add in sugar substitute. Even to me there is no difference in the taste, but the very idea of having to go through this because of diabetes is frustrating. I'm starting to hate the word sugar.

"It's been almost a year and a half. The time has only led to situations to being worse. I'm not happy." I add three packets of sugar substitute.

"You think about transferring schools?" He asks.

"It's always an option," I say. "I've never considered it though."

"Well, do what you have to do to take care of yourself kid."

I don't what to talk about it anymore. I stir my coffee to blend all the condiments together. "We should get going. Don't want to be late for another exciting day."

The week before exams approaches quickly and catches me off guard. It is a Sunday night, and I have my first-semester exams on Monday, Tuesday, and Wednesday. Everything going on in life is still in the chaotic mess I have created. The ex-girlfriend and I continue to argue about our relationship, grades are maintaining at a D average, my health is getting to be at an all-time low, and the depression is sinking in deeper internally. Happiness is nowhere to around and once again I am trapped in the dark maze of compulsive thinking and depressed state of mind.

My mother calls for me to come downstairs to discuss something. When I make my way downstairs, I see my parents and younger brother sitting at the kitchen table.

"We need to talk about your schooling," my mother says.

"What about it?" I ask.

"Well, your grades have been suffering and show no signs of improvement. Do you think your grades could improve?"

I am trying to find reasons to say yes. Maybe everything could improve. Maybe I can work harder. Maybe the relationships with friends will get better. As hard as I attempt to find a reason to stay I come up empty.

"No mom," I replied. "There isn't."

"Your brother thinks you should go to his school." My mother says as she gestures towards my younger brother.

I look over to him and say, "Tell me about it."

"It's a good school," He says to me. "Teachers help you out and there are a lot of nice kids there. Plus some of your good friends already go there."

"A.J.," my mom says. "We can schedule an appointment with a guidance counselor at school talk about transferring." A silence settles in. "What do you think?"

I think for a moment. This dilemma is put right in front of me, and I only have a couple of minutes to decide. I already have my decision made up.

"Make the arrangements for me to transfer."

As I walk away towards the stairs, my father motions me to stop. He pauses for a moment and speaks. "It may be rough at first, but you'll pull through it."

I appreciate his encouraging words and silently go up the stairs to my room.

I sit in bed and think about the dilemma of transferring schools. It comes down to the choice of either staying and more than likely failing or moving to a different one and starting all over. I know my parents and brother want to me transfer. In the end, the decision is mine to make, and I took the decision to transfer.

I think for a moment about everything I have done to my parents with all of this mess. I have kept them in the dark with so many issues and directly lied to them about issues regarding my health. I waste their time taking me to appointments that don't matter. I waste their money on medications that I don't use and throw away. Nothing to be proud of and only disappointment to live with a son who has a chronic illness and nothing else.

Maybe transferring will be something I can at least do for them. Maybe a different scene could be the answer to all the misery going on. The decision to transfer schools doesn't feel real at first. It seems so unreal that for the first two days of exams I don't tell anyone at school I am leaving. I keep secrets, and I lie. I lie about coming back and keep the secret about transferring. I walk through the halls and into my classrooms like nothing is wrong. I go to school these days and act as if I am going to return the next semester. The final day his me with the truth; I'm leaving.

It's the last night of being a student at this school. I start letting some people know, and most of the responses are mostly "good luck" and nothing else. It becomes easier because after only a few of those responses it becomes clear that telling some people will not serve any purpose. But, I know I have to tell some of the guys that I take to school and the close friends I do have.

My final exam is over, and I have no other responsibilities as a student here. I am leaving everything behind, and I don't intend on bringing anything with me, except maintaining the only friendships I have. I still haven't told anyone else I am leaving this school and never coming back. By the end of the day, I pack up everything from my locker and make my way towards the exit.

In my viewpoint, I notice an old friend on my way out. As I pass her, I feel like stopping and telling her everything about what happened between us and the fact that I am leaving. I want to stop and tell her I want our friendship like it was in the past. Part of me begins to think maybe there is another chance at this place. Perhaps giving it another shot would be best. But nothing is said. Something keeps me going, pushing me along, and preventing me from stopping. I walk right past her, get into my car, and drive off for the last time as a student here.

Halfway driving home I start to cry uncontrollably. I don't know why this is happening. Transferring is supposed to be beneficial to me. Transferring is meant to be the right choice to make. I am expected to be able to look back and think the decision to leave is the right one, and my ability to handle a stressful situation is proven without a doubt. I think transferring is the right move to make, and the decision is going to help me get my life back on track. All of the sudden I start having these thoughts of panic and worry. They aren't the compulsive thoughts and questions I can't answer. These are thoughts of regret and almost disbelief.

I start to think about my friendships with people at school, and even the friendships I didn't have with people. I say to myself how much I wish I could have been friends with some people that I never knew. On the way back, I start contemplating my reason for not telling anyone I was leaving. I think my decision to withhold my information about transferring is the fact that I can't bring it to myself to tell people, which I am afraid to.

I start to realize I didn't want to tell them. The whole time I thought if I told everyone I was transferring people would give me the guilt trip about leaving. I don't want to hear people explain they want me to stay, or they can't believe I am going. People at school would have been talking to me more, now that I am leaving, instead of when I was there as a fellow student.

I go home today and sat in bed staring at the ceiling all night. I stare at the ceiling and attempt to make sense at everything going on. The maze appears again, and I am stuck there trying to find my way out. All the questions and compulsive thoughts lead me deeper and deeper into the maze and distancing myself even further from finding my way out.

Most of the night and the following day, I spend alone. I keep a distance from everyone and don't talk to anyone from either school. I isolate myself and for some reason want to be left alone. No one from the new school knows I am going to be transferring their next semester. Maybe this is the fresh start I need. Wipe the slate clean. Start from scratch. Perhaps this change in scenery will be the opportunity I am desperately looking for to make some difference. By making the transition, and leave everything behind, maybe this will be exactly what I need.

CHAPTER 8

Wherever I Go, the Misery Will Follow

"You cannot escape the responsibility of tomorrow by evading it today."

Quote Inspired by Abraham Lincoln

This new found source of relief is comforting. Having the comfort and support of friends provides me with confidence and security when the first day at this new school begins. Even though I have more confidence and relief, I don't want to set myself up for failure. I don't expect to make a lot of new friends or fit in right away. A grade school friend guides me around to most of the classes. Instead of being stuck with a locker near the freshman, the school allows me to share a locker with two close friends.

As I walk through the hallways I am amazed to see all the faces I know. Since I hanging out with some of my friends from this school, I often saw these people on the weekends. I don't know them at first, but now that I attend to the same school as them I am making the connection. Inside I feel as if I know more people here than I did at the previous place. For a short time, I start feeling like I belong somewhere. I have a feeling inside of me that everything is working, and the pieces are falling into place. Fitting in and leaving all the insecurities and misery about my diabetes behind me is starting to become more visible.

One of the biggest differences that stand out is seeing my brother more often. It is strange to think about at first because my sister attended the previous school I was at during my freshman year. Whether it was our schedules or my tendency to isolate, I did not see her that often. I remember her driving me home at times and seeing me in the hallway. It's hard hiding things from your siblings, and a part of me always had an instinct that she knew I was miserable. My younger brother was the first person to tell me they wanted me at this school. He sat, at the table with my parents, and said he wanted me to be there.

Hearing that was heartfelt and yet emotionally draining at the same time. I am the older brother and should be the one to help him through his early years in school and be the strong one of the two. It feels shameful to think I was not strong enough to get through what happened at school and be the role model for him. At the same time, I didn't know who else to look up to right now. Telling this to your older brother in front of your parents had to take a lot of courage. I could have responded to him a lot differently, but I knew right away by his conviction at such a young age that he wanted me there.

I keep walking through the halls in search of faces, classroom numbers, bathrooms, and all the familiar surroundings in school. A surprise comes around the corner when I spot a neighborhood friend down the hall. We have been best friends since he moved into the neighborhood. I never had an older brother, so became the neighborhood brother How did I forget about him? How did I not think about him going here? It becomes quite clear how lost I had become with even the people who I consider to be close. Stuck in my head left me neglecting even the closest people that I did have. Close enough to having only three houses separate us.

The school and nursing staff was immediately made aware of the condition of my health and everything required to manage the diabetes. All of the insulin, syringes, test strips, and blood meter are stored in the nurse's office. Instead of being excused from class to come down it was my responsibility to show up before lunch. The relieving part about this school is that the nurse's office is on the way to the lunchroom, so it didn't feel like I have to go off to some random room somewhere in the building.

Managing diabetes is a lot easier when other people are aware of what you need to do. I come into the office and immediately let the nurse on duty know I am taking my blood sugar. After notifying them of the level, it is documented in a binder with all my information. Then, I draw up the insulin and let them know how much I am taking. That again is documented. Finally, they witness me taking the insulin injection to ensure it was being done.

Nothing about it felt great. The finger pokes and insulin injections still hurt and bother me. The constant need to take my blood sugar and count carbohydrates is still annoying. But, I have to admit it is better than having to hide in a bathroom stall. No more keeping the syringes and insulin vials in a rolled up brown paper bag. It feels good not having to carry it around me like a dirty little secret. I can keep it in the nurse's office where some people know about it and for right now I am okay with that.

These simple things are a good start to helping with the insecurities with diabetes. I feel as if I can leave it there and not carry it around everywhere I go. Dealing with it for a few short moments is better than having it with me all the time and dealing with the constant back and forth questions about whether or not to even take my insulin. I find it easier to go back to thinking about getting accustomed to the new classes, new teachers, and new students. It starts to become easier to forget about everything that happened before and focus on what is going on right now.

All of the sudden the plan backfires and hits me straight on. I didn't realize at first when I made the transfer I was going to be attending the same school that my ex-girlfriend attends. How could this have completely gone over my head? When my family mentioned the school her name did not come to mind. When I thought about talking to people and telling them about my decision, a thought never appeared to tell me maybe I should let her know. I didn't even think about the first few days until a mutual friend asks me if I had seen her yet.

A wave of horrible memories floods back in. I forget about looking for the classroom numbers and talking to other students. I start recalling everything that was going on during that entire ordeal. The break-up, the arguing, the depression, the concerns, the worries, the doubts, the fears, and the misery. I think back to the days at school where I didn't know what I was doing or where I was going. The feeling of that old reality is starting to combine with the fact of today.

It starts to feel unfamiliar and almost like being in her territory. I have no clue what I would say to her, so I start doing what I do best and begin to keep myself distant. For the first week or two I don't see her and avoid making any attempt at communicating with her. However, in a school where two people know each other it's nearly impossible to believe I will never run into her. When I see her again, some of the old feelings and emotions start coming back. As hard as I try to hide or escape from the feelings and emotions I know it won't work. We are back where we were before; arguing and fighting at any chance we get.

Everyone knows what is going on between us and this is no secret. She makes our relationship worse when she decides to go out with another guy whom I don't have a good past with. With her the fighting and arguing never ends. We continue to talk on the phone and see each other, but our relationship never improves. The arguing is a constant tug of rope war. We go back and forth hurting one another, dragging other people into the fight, and making the whole situation worse.

The misery and depression I wanted to leave behind follows me to my new school. The same feelings start to creep up inside of me; feelings of being different and a lost sense of belonging. My behavior among other students resembles that of my old school. I start avoiding conversations and contact with fellow students. I want to come to school, complete my classes and go home.

I start contemplating whether or not transferring was the right decision or not. I can't believe it; the decision that was supposed to be beneficial and provide me with the help I need has failed. Wiping the slate clean and starting over was a letdown; because apparently the same writing is staying on the walls. Once again, I begin to feel different. I feel dirty, and I feel disgusting.

I don't know what to do at this point. And it's no surprise because I didn't know what to do at the other school either. For the most part, I try and stick to the friends I do have and try not to focus on anything else going on. But surely enough, the insecurities begin to affect my diabetes. It was easier to hide, avoid and neglect the health issues before because the school did not know about it. But here, that is a different story.

They know about my health and have a system in place to keep track of everything. But as the days were getting more and more frustrating it became harder to want to go there. Each time I made my way towards the nurse's office I had the desire to keep walking right passed it and head to lunch. I find more and more reasons to think about forgetting it, doing later, and that I'll be fine this one time without it.

The more and more I think about it, and the emotions of being frustrated, disappointed, and angry make it easier to get to the point where I start skipping taking my insulin again. All the contemplating, arguing, and debating finally leads back to just saying forget it, and walking straight to lunch. Friends ask about me going, and I look them right in the face and lie about how the nurse's office was.

Completing skipping my insulin does not work for long. The school was smarter than I gave them credit for, and they began tracking me down after a few times of missing going to the nurse. It is to the point where they have a student come to the classroom, hand a note to the teacher, and have the teacher instruct me to go to the nurse's office in the middle of class. Feels like all eyes are on me, and everyone is thinking about my diabetes. The nurses accept the "I forgot" excuse but make it clear they are expecting to see me every day before lunch.

You would think when I was caught it would put an end to the lying and avoiding. But the feelings of frustration, anger, and irritation only led to a stronger desire to find new ways I could stop having to take insulin injections and finger pokes. If I couldn't simply walk past the nurse's office, then the only other choice was to manipulate my way while in there. So I start lying about how high my blood sugars are and even lie about taking my blood in the first place. I begin to go through the motions of getting all the medical supplies necessary and pretend to do it. I place the blood strip in the meter, set the lancet and press down on air and not my finger. I wait ten seconds and pretend to read a number from the machine.

Same thing for taking my insulin injections. I pretend to pull out a new syringe from the packet. I draw it back and pretend to push it into the vial of insulin only to carefully place it right next to it. Then I pretend to inject myself even to the point of making a grimace on my face to sell it to the nurse. I quickly place everything back into the medical bag, thank the nurse, and make my way to the lunchroom with everyone else.

Lying to the nurses is never something I enjoyed doing. But it is easier in my head to say it's none of their business, and they would not want to have to poke or inject themselves with needles all day. However, it is all the more gut wrenching when one of the nurses is my aunt. Most of the time, I take my insulin when she is in there compared to a different nurse. On the days when I am more frustrated or upset I still lie to her. She trusts me when I tell her what my blood sugar is and how many units of insulin I take. She knows of my situation transferring to this school and wants to see me do good, and I don't want to disappoint her by telling her how nothing has improved.

I wonder what would happen if she asks me and instead of lying to her about it I would explain the truth. How would she respond if I told her that I don't want to take my meds? How would she react if I told her that insulin injections hurt? What would she do if I told her that I felt miserable simply coming here every single day? But it takes courage to say that to someone. And because I am absent of courage right now it makes it easier to fall back on the lying, manipulating, hiding, escaping, and avoiding.

Getting away with it the first time only set a precedent to keep trying even more. It feels right not having to poke my finger with a sharp object or stab myself with a needle. At that moment, I get to escape the pain and discomfort of diabetes and move on. But moving on never actually happens. The effects of not taking my blood sugar or insulin injections begin to settle in once again. Concentrating in school becomes more and more difficult. I feel sluggish and lethargic most of the time. I have to excuse myself to go to the bathroom because of the frequent urination and rush during breaks between classes at times.

It is easier now to avoid and neglect everything about my diabetes. Unfortunately, it also becomes easier to lie to my parents about how everything at school is going. I don't want to disappoint them and make them feel as if they made a poor choice to recommend a transfer to another school that was not working out for me. *What would they do? What would they think of me?*

I justify inside my head that pretending everything is going well is better for them, so they do not have to worry or doubt themselves.

They have been through enough with me since this all started. The hospitals, doctors, nurses, health insurance, pharmacies, late nights staying up with me as a kid, and everything else that involves having a child with a chronic illness. I do not want to hurt them any more than I have so it's better if I keep everything going on inside and act like everything on the outside is going just fine.

So the motions keep going and everything seems just as it was before. Only this time I do not see going to another school as an escape hatch or way out. Finding support is a little harder, because sometimes talking to my friends meant questions regarding my health or asking about how everything is going between me and the ex-girlfriend. Intramural basketball starts at my old grade school. Basketball in the past provided me with a sense of belonging, positive role in my life, stress relief, and a form of healthy recreation that benefited my diabetes.

Basketball is not the same anymore. Everything it did in the past was not giving me the same advantages in the present. The excitement and purpose driven feelings are not there. The fans are not there, talking about it at school does not happen, and life is not changing because of it. I still do it because when I get out there on the court I get to remember what it was like before. Playing in the same gym as I did before and standing on the same court I did in the better days provided a relief that going to school or going home did not provide.

I also do not see the need to take care of my diabetes in order to make sure basketball goes well. Since school is not improving, and the health is slowly deteriorating, it is no surprise that basketball is suffering. The mental frustration and physical exhaustion caused by high blood sugars make running up and down the court and being an efficient player almost an impossible task.

One day at school, I head to the nurse's office to most likely lie about my number and pretend to take another injection. Before going in, the ex-girlfriend stops in front of my locker, and it turns quickly into another series of disagreements. As she leaves, a friend notices and asks how that went. I don't want to talk about it and begin to walk away. He reminds me to go to the nurse's office and offers to go with me. Instead of saying, "that's nice and I'd appreciate the support" or "it would feel good to have someone there" I decide to let frustration and anger answer for me. I keep walking and say back over my shoulder, "I don't need someone watching me."

I head to the nurse's office to get this over with, so I can get through the day and head to practice. I was looking forward to shooting hoops and being around some of the basketball players. As soon as I enter the room the nurse follows me over to the counter and observes me going through the diabetes management. Why can't they just leave me alone? Why do they have to watch me? Having them next to me is not comforting at all. But, instead of fighting the ordeal I decide to move forward.

I take my blood, and it is well over two hundred. The nurse responds by saying, "Isn't that kind of high?" I can read the blood glucose meter, and I am well aware that over two hundred is high. This is not something I want to be reminded of by someone who does not have diabetes. So I measure out the units of insulin for lunch and add the extra units to make up for the high blood level. The injection goes in and is immediately painful. I pull the syringe out and notice insulin and a little blood coming out.

Even when I attempt to take care of my diabetes something has to go wrong. Having insulin come back out is a moment when you want just to throw everything away and say, "What the hell do you want from me diabetes?" You can't measure out the insulin that did not go in, and there is no guarantee any of the insulin that did go in is going to work. So what can I do? I can sit and wait, test my blood again later, and then most likely give myself another injection. I hate doing this process once and what makes you think I am going to want to do it again right away?

The rest of the day is no picnic either. I get an update on my grades and see they are not going well and are starting to slip. My academics are not as bad as before, but they are not something to be proud of either. I just want to get to basketball and have this day over with. Practice is going horribly wrong. I can't make a shot in the world tonight, and everything negative about my life is inside my head. Tonight I can't shake the thoughts out of my mind.

Not only is the mental part being a distraction but I can feel the physical effects of having a high blood sugar. I can barely make it up and down the court without feeling sluggish. I stay later than everyone else because I am hoping that as soon as more buckets start to go in the negative thoughts will get out. But that doesn't happen, and the irritability and frustration finally win. I tell myself this will be the final shot I take for the night. If I make this three then maybe that will be a good sign for tomorrow. The ball doesn't even get close to going in, and as I walk past the hoop I throw my fist into the back of the gymnasium wall. The punch tears the skin off three of my knuckles causing them to bleed all over and eventually bruise.

I get into my car and see there is a missed call and voice message. As I look at the number, it surprises me to see the ex-girlfriend is the one who called. I hesitate for a second and consider closing the phone and not calling back. But I don't. I pick up the phone and call her back.

"Hey," I say to her.

"Hi. What are you up to?" She asks.

"Nothing much. Just got done with basketball practice."

"How was it?"

"Eh. Same old, same old." I respond.

"Want to come over and talk for a little while? I know it is late, but just for a short time."

"Sure," I say. "I'm on my way."

"Alright. I'll see you soon," and she hangs up.

As I drive to her house, I have no idea what to expect or what will come out of this conversation. At first I don't even know why I agree to come over in the first place. I accepted immediately without even thinking about it. I know if I go home I will probably be up all night having curiosity driving me crazy. So I think to myself what could be the worst that could happen? I pull into her driveway, and before I put my car in park she comes out of the front door, makes her way to the car, opens the passenger door, and takes a seat.

"Hey there," she says, as a smile comes across her face.

"Hi," I respond, looking in the other direction to avoid making eye contact.

Before an ordinary conversation has time to accumulate, she notices the blood and torn skin on the knuckles of my right hand.

"What happened to your hand?" she asks in a half concern, half anger voice.

"Nothing. Basketball practice didn't go as well as usual." I respond.

"Did you hit somebody?"

"No, no, no. I punched the back wall on the way out of the gym."

"Why?"

"Because," I respond. "Practice wasn't going well and I was playing terrible."

"Is it because we argued before you had practice today by your locker?"

"I don't know," I respond, using a tone that lets her know I don't want to talk about it.

"You shouldn't have hurt yourself," she says. "That's not like you."

After she says that we sit there in silence. I think about what she said when she remarked "that's not like you." I don't know who I am or what I am doing in my life. My thinking gets interrupted as she speaks.

"I should get going. It's getting late, and we have school tomorrow."

"Alright," I respond.

"I'll see you tomorrow. Take care of yourself."

Before I have time to respond, she closes the door behind her and walks into her house. I drive home and thoughts are racing through my head again. I didn't want to go back. I want to talk to her and end this fighting between us. To be truthful, she wasn't on my mind during practice or what caused the frustration. I was still mad at her for everything that had occurred, so a part of me wanted her to feel that. But, I didn't punch the wall because of her. I hit the door because life wasn't the same as it was before when I was happy. And diabetes was the reason.

It would have taken courage to tell her that none of this was really about us and that everything had to do with the struggles of my health. But once again, courage is something still absent in my character. Instead, she opened the door and said it was because of us arguing, and I decided to manipulate, blame, and make excuses to convince her she was the cause.

She became an easy scapegoat for all of my problems. It's wrong of me to do it, but part of me feels justified because of how things between me and her went down. I am okay with it because in my head I tell myself that other people should hurt as much as I do. There is nothing courageous about that. I know deep down all of this has nothing to do with her but my courage to admit that and do something about it is obsolete.

The biggest problem with my health is the fact I am not taking care of it, and I still have not found a way to coexist happily with the condition of diabetes on a daily basis. Even though, I can lie and trick the health room nurses once in a while, they always document my blood glucose levels and monitor me while injecting myself with insulin. I still get away with giving false blood levels and pretending to inject insulin, but I can't do it all the time. Even so, the health room nurses are only around during lunch. This leaves breakfast, dinner, and nighttime the perfect opportunities to neglect my health.

Avoiding people was a lot easier at my previous school. Here, it is a lot harder. Even when I try and stay isolated or avoid talking to people, there are a good amount who actively continue to support what is going on. One friend, a guy with a sarcastic sense of humor, provides me with the help of listening and analyzing the thoughts and feelings that are compulsively racing through my head. Whenever I need to, I can call him and talk about anything.

It becomes a habit for us, and we decide to make it a weekly ritual of going to Starbucks, ordering two caramel apple ciders, and having discussions about life in general. My sister is working at Starbucks now, and it is comforting to see her there behind the counter while I am spending time with a friend. For some reason today I think about what it was like going to school with her for that short period. I wonder if she knew I was miserable at that school. I wonder if she knew I wasn't happy and that I dreaded each day. Either way, seeing her now brings warmth.

I sit down with my good friend and this particular discussion we have is about the ex-girlfriend.

"What's on your mind?" He asks before he takes a sip of hot caramel apple cider.

"Same old, same old" I respond.

"You thinking about her?"

"Yeah, a little bit."

"How did it go the other night when you mentioned stopping over there?"

"Brief. I don't even know why I went over there. Part of me just wants to act like all of this is behind me and have everyone else do the same thing."

"That's going to be a little hard to do because you know how people are," he says.

Part of the frustration is that everyone does talk about it and ask how it is going almost on a regular basis. People are either asking how I am doing or how she is doing or how we both are doing with the entire ordeal. Sometimes I feel like it is more of an entertainment purpose for people than it is something I care to address. At the same time, it is easier for everyone to focus on that instead of talking about something no one has a clue about it.

"Well, that's fine with me."

"What's fine with you?" He asks.

"Nothing, man. I'm just rambling." I brush it off like it's nothing and don't want to get into the other things, the main things that are going on. I should tell him that it's got nothing to do with her. I should tell a lot of people that it does not have to do with her. There were a lot of things going on at first, but after some time it became less about being at the same school with her and more about all the frustration of dealing with my diabetes. Maybe if I told him, he would tell others, and then the gossiping, drama aspects of the entire thing would be over. But, that would take more courage.

Silence settles in as I put both hands around the apple cider, and I glare directly at the cup.

"Let's move along," I say to him, not wanting to talk about her anymore. "You brought some writings you worked on. Let's talk about those."

We don't always find answers when we have these talks, but that doesn't matter. All of my friends provide some support I need at this time. It is strange to notice that with the strong support network I have I am still incapable of breaking through my depression and solving my deeper troubles. Despite the negative attitude and depressing behaviors, my friends never give up on me.

At this point, I still don't care. I don't have the courage, strength, or self-determination to want to make a change in my life despite everything happening. Instead, I continue going in the same direction I have been going; further and further into the dark maze of misery.

I walk around the halls at school with my head down and think nothing of the surroundings. The thoughts and compulsive questions continuously race around in my head without the final flag being waved to stop them. They are out of control and everything I try to do just screams failure. A failure to solve my problems, a failure to achieve in my academics, a failure to take proper care of my health, and a failure to those who care about me. I am a failure.

The days start to blur together again. I go bed and want to sleep. I want to wake up realize all of this is one big nightmare. The compulsive thoughts are racing inside my head without any control. My eyes get heavy and before I know it I fall asleep. All of the sudden my eyes open and I can feel my mom struggling to put a Wisconsin Badgers sweatshirt over my shoulders and before I know it.

DARKNESS again. I manage to open my eyes again. At this point, my mom is carrying me through two automatic doors that read emergency room in red letters. Again, my head is spinning, my vision is blurry, and before I know it…

DARKNESS. I open my eyes, and I am lying down in an ambulance, looking through the windows. Through the small window, I can see the hospital sitting on top of the hill. For the last time, my head is spinning, and my vision turns pitch black and I am unconscious. I wake up, and I am sweating. I am in my bed at home. It is another nightmare, another flashback of what happened to me that day.

I sit at the end of my bed with my hands covering my face. I hate these nightmares; I hate these reoccurring thoughts. There is a lot of tension building up inside of me, and I have to release it in some way. It is six in the morning, and I put on my basketball shoes and go downstairs in the basement. My father is out of town on business and I decide to run on the treadmill.

I run because of the tension built up inside of me. I have anger and hate for the nightmares and flashbacks of that horrible day. I slowly walk, but the pace begins to increase. The more anger and

71

hate I have the faster and faster I decide to run. My legs start to hurt, but it doesn't matter. I keep running and running. The pain doesn't matter to me, and I push to keep going further and further. It feels like my legs are burning with fire. I think more and more about the pain associated with my diabetes and it fuels the fire to continue running. I continue to run and run, more and more until I finally stop because I feel like I can't even physically run anymore.

I go to school, and nothing changes. I avoid making any attempt at communicating with most peers unless they initiate the conversation. Concentrating in school is impossible, and the thought of getting good grades and accomplishing in academics is lost. I don't make any new friends and socializing with students at school is only thought. I just want the day to end so I can go home. At home, the anxiety acts up. I start to feel antsy, move around, and cannot keep still. Nothing is helping, and I need to get out of the house, so I call my sarcastic friend to come pick me up.

"How are you doing good sir?" He asks as I get into the front seat.

"The usual," I say. He probably knows by now the usual is never a good response.

"Where to?" he asks.

"Where do you think?"

"Starbucks it is."

"I got something for ya," I say as I reach into my pocket and pull out a jewel case with a compact disc in it. I open it up and slip it into the stereo.

"What's this?"

"Thinking mix, first one," I respond.

"Thinking mix, huh?"

"Yeah. It helps me out."

"Sounds like a good idea to me. You've got some good songs here."

"Keep it. It's your copy."

Sometimes I wish the music on the disc would tell him everything going on inside my head. I wish it could explain what is going on regarding my health, the depression, and the anxiety. It would be a lot easier for someone else to tell it and say it as opposed to me having to do it. After he hears it maybe someone else could listen then. And maybe after so many times listening to it something could finally be different. All I know at this point is I am nowhere near feeling close to talking about any of it.

CHAPTER 9

When Comfort Becomes Destructive

"Beware a dagger hidden in a smile."

Quote Inspired by Shi Nai'an, Ming Dynasty

Life isn't getting much worse, but it isn't getting any better either. And this is a weird spot to be in. Like being stuck right in the middle of no man's land. Knowing you cannot go back, but not knowing where you are going in the future. The holiday break is approaching, and I am eager to have this opportunity to be away from it all. Although the holidays are not as enjoyable anymore as a diabetic. Most of the time, it becomes a steady reminder of all the food people tell me I can't eat or am not supposed to eat because I can't have sugar. And with a holiday season like Christmas it is nearly impossible not be surrounded by sugary cookies.

With all the drama and pain going on I need something to look forward to; be excited about. Christmas passes, New Year's Eve is approaching, and a friend of mine is having a small gathering at his house. There are only a few of us there, no more than ten. Most of my friends want to drink tonight. At this point in my life, I have never consumed alcohol, and I never really have any reason to do so. Every time my friends drink I take the role of the caretaker. I watch over everyone and make sure no one is drinking too much or putting themselves in any potential danger.

A friend of mine brought a bottle of Champaign to celebrate the New Year. He asks me if I want to make a toast to celebrate. At first, I hesitate but then think, "what the hell, why not," and I have my first drink. The first drink I have is to celebrate a new year, a new beginning. Ever since everything from the previous school went sour to transferring here where all the misery followed. The first drink commences a new life to begin, one without suffering or pain. So I drink the glass of Champaign, and it brings a sense of relief and feelings of potential change.

Out of all the possible ways to describe how it felt, the best way is to simply say it felt good. But the drink in it of itself was not good strangely enough. What felt right was feeling like I was doing something everyone else was a part of. Being included, part of the group, and almost like a silent "there you go" from everyone else there. It was only one drink, and that was it – and yet it gives me a sense of satisfaction and enjoyment.

All of the sudden my cell phone is ringing. A friend is calling, we chit chat for a few seconds, and I extend the invite to come over to the party. As soon as they arrive some of us decide to go to the nearby grocery store to pick up some food to bring back. A few of us gather in my friend's car and head over. When we return to the small gathering, we notice the host's father pulling up in the driveway in his truck. We immediately turn around and drive in the opposite direction. For whatever reason, two of my friends suggest going to the ex-girlfriend's house to hang out there.

I am opposed to the whole idea from the start. We are still on the rocks and the last thing I want to do at the moment is go over and see her. We argued earlier in the day, and I know she is having her boyfriend and some other friends over for New Year's. When we pull into her driveway, I know this is a bad idea. I stay near the car as a friend goes up to the doorbell. The other two friends remain in the car, and I can't help but wonder why out of all places my friends decide to come to this house.

My friend rings the doorbell and after a few minutes the ex-girlfriend opens the front door. When she opens the door, she looks over at me, and we make eye contact. I don't want to be here, and I don't want to see her at this moment. Just a few moments before we were all having fun and now it is coming to a halt. My friend explains to her what happened to us at the house. In the midst of telling the story, I hear my friend telling her that I am extremely drunk and out of control. I look back at my two friends in the car and almost start laughing at his remarks. As soon as I turn back around she comes right up and slaps me across the face. At first, I am dumbfounded after trying to comprehend what just happened.

I am not even drunk, let alone feeling any effects of the alcohol, and I was slapped across the face. She has this look on her face like I should know better. Forget my friend who is entirely intoxicated, but focus on me because what I did was wrong. Almost like I was not allowed to drink but it was okay for everyone else to do that. Why does she have such a problem with me having a drink anyways? I know she has consumed alcohol. What makes it wrong for me to do that when she can and so can everyone else? She must think I can't do it because it is unhealthy for my diabetes. Another thing that is apparently something I cannot do.

At first it is all about fitting in and doing what everyone else was doing. Strange how normal it is to go directly to a party over the weekend, have a few drinks and feel like you were doing what everyone else was doing. Dealing with the insecurities and compulsive thoughts is much easier after consuming a couple of alcoholic beverages. It's definitely easier to be one of the drunks than it is the stand alone diabetic.

As fast as the alcohol helps with the destructive thinking it easily wears off nearly just as quickly. Before I know it, the thoughts are right back there except being more chaotic and irrational. Even when I am sitting down with others, I find ways to think of myself as being different and not like the rest. Then it becomes easier for me to isolate even when I am surrounded by plenty of people. I find my way to being near the corners in the room, on the edge of couches, and make my way towards rooms where fewer people are socializing. When people are by me, I become more silent and easily use the alcoholic beverage to maintain some comfort.

The more uncomfortable I feel in these situations the more tempting it becomes to reach out to that drink to try and cope. If the insecurities and self-doubts would not go away, the best next approach is to be tipsy while dealing with them. Back at the old high school I was upset and hurt by the fact I never went to the parties or social gatherings. Now, I am here, and yet I still find some reason to be disappointed. Not good enough when I'm not there, not good enough while I am here. What kind of sense does that make?

The drinking and diabetes are not the best mixes either. With one or two drinks, at first, it's not a combination that becomes concerning. The two biggest mistakes I was getting good at, unfortunately, was not eating while drinking and then eating while drinking. Sometimes I would not eat any food so my blood sugar would not go sky high on me while at a party. So, in order to avoid this happening, I would drink more alcohol and eat much less food.

Drinking more on an empty stomach always helps the alcohol hit you more. Then there are the times where I would get so intoxicated to the point where I wouldn't care and eat the entire kitchen sink. When parties had a dozen pizzas and snacks all over, I wouldn't hesitate to consume anything that I wanted. All or nothing thinking led to going to the extremes on both ends.

What made matters even worse was never bringing any of my diabetic supplies with me. Do you think I am going to come to a party with my blood meter and test strips? I don't even take my injections on an average basis at home so why would I bring my syringes and insulin to a party? There is no way I am going to bring this here when I fake it half the time at the nurse's office. No way am I going to bring the diabetic misery into these situations.

These are the opportunities to forget all about the diabetes, the school worries, and be able to do what everyone else is doing. No blood meter, finger pokes, counting carbohydrates, insulin bottles, and injections with syringes. More eating whatever I want, whenever I want, and drinking what I want with the other peers. This feels more normal and comforting even in misery.

Certain times of embarrassment are even more sympathetic than worrying. Falling over, throwing up, or saying something unrecognizable due to the help of alcohol was a more common experience than high blood sugars, measuring insulin and finding a new spot to inject me. People can laugh and relate to the struggles of walking up a flight of stairs under the influence a lot more in comparison to the worry and fear of seeing insulin and blood coming out of a recent injection site.

Drinking is something I see as being able to do and not care about. Since the beginning of the diagnosis, I was constantly being told what I can and cannot do. "You can't eat sugar. You can't go without insulin. You aren't like the rest of everyone else. You can't go right to lunch. You can't eat before taking your blood levels. You can't take your blood on the table where the food is. You can't eat any of the snacks because of the sugar." I was even told about certain careers or jobs I couldn't do because of my condition.

Alcohol, in a very harmful way, gave plenty of reasons to throw in the towel and not care about any of those things anymore. I didn't care about what I wasn't supposed to do and just simply did it. If other peers can than so can I, and that gives me a sense of entitlement even when it means placing my health at risk. I want to drink and drink to the point where my thinking leaves me alone. I don't wish to talk about what is going on in my life, and the insecurities hidden beneath the damaging behaviors and self destructing thoughts. When friends want to know what's going on it's easy to avoid it by just redirecting them on the upcoming weekend of drinking.

Alcohol does a lot for me, or so I think. It becomes a friend. Never does it turn me down, judge me, or let me down. Every time I want to drink the alcohol is there for me. My alcohol abuse also provides me with other benefits besides being a companion. Consuming alcohol stops the compulsive thinking. Whenever my negative thinking starts acting up, I take a shot of vodka and the thoughts stop. The focus and attention are more on the act of drinking and consuming the alcohol instead of my negative thoughts.

I know the drinking is starting to worry my friends. Before I started drinking, I would be the one to take care of others. People were having fun, laughing, and enjoying things. But it was different from the start when I drink. Friends are more concerned, have a more watchful eye, and rarely drink when I am. So taking turns would be a regular part of the pattern. One weekend night it would be their turn, the next day would be mine, and then back to school and diabetes for further misery.

Another appointment with the hospital and doctor approaches. I spend most of the day at school figuring out how I am going to approach this. Should I say I left my meter at home or school? Should I tell them that there is a second blood meter I am using so the one I bring to the appointment is only partially full? Do I falsify the blood sugar levels in my log or entirely say I forgot that as well? What did I do last time? What is the chance the doctor is going to remember what I said last time?

I walk in and hate going through the same old doors that remind me each and every time of what happened on that horrible day. The nurse greets me and asks for my blood meter. I pretend to look in my bag and lie about leaving it in my locker. I tell the nurse I was in such a hurry from staying late at school to work on homework, and then rush to the hospital for my appointment that I completely forgot about double checking to see where my supplies were. What she doesn't know is that I left school right away and spent the entire time driving around trying to figure out what lies I was going to tell her.

Getting passed her was easy, but the doctor can be another story. I'm a little nervous sitting in there thinking the doctor is going to catch me lying. I imagine both of them talking outside of the office about not having any of my supplies and wasting their time, money, and resources. The door opens and in comes a doctor whom I have never met before. This makes it a lot easier.

The nurse already explained to the doctor my reason (excuse) for not bringing the supplies. She reminds me about the importance of having all of this stuff with me during appointments. Strange how there is no discussion about having it on me all the time. You would think if I forgot it during an important meeting there would be a higher likelihood this "forgetting" would be a common practice for me. But, a simple reminder from the doctor and the appointment continues. She asks the usual questions regarding the date I was diagnosed, age, and the usual boring questions they should already have written down.

I leave the hospital and toss the reminder appointment card in a trash bin on the way out. Sometimes it is easier to say I lost the appointment card and completely miss an appointment. At least I don't have to come back here again for another three to four months or even longer if I decide to forget about going.

The school week goes by like a blur and the weekend approaches. A group of friends and I choose to attend a local church festival where I went to grade school. The festival is held at our old grade and is one of the most enjoyable activities we looked forward to as kids. At the end of the school year, we would see the trucks and trailers pull in to set up the rides and games. I used to go on rides with friends and hang out with the basketball teammates. But, over the past two years it has become more stressful and anxiety provoking than anything.

Before we get there, I decide to drink a water bottle of vodka. The festival is about five minutes from the house, so I decide to drink on the walk there. It takes us about twenty minutes to get there and as I walk around the school grounds I am already intoxicated. The night starts out on a rough note from the very beginning. Immediately I notice some people from my old school. Eye contact and a few head nods are communicated to us, and nothing else transpires. No one comes over to greet me or see how I am doing, and I don't go over to them either.

The night becomes even more uncomfortable and dreadful as the unimaginable happens. After walking around for a while, I notice the ex-girlfriend with her boyfriend. She decides to approach me and lecture me about my drinking and what I am doing to myself. My friends decide to step in and interrupt by starting a conversation with her. This gives me the chance to remove myself from the situation. Immediately afterward, her boyfriend comes over and starts talking to me. It didn't take a detective to notice the act he is putting on and acting sarcastically like we are friends.

He put his arm around my shoulder and makes a remark about being buddies. He laughs and smiles over near his friends who are right nearby. I look towards my friends and see their backs turned as they continue to talk with the ex-girlfriend. He continues to make comments and laugh them off. It feels degrading. Almost like a young child being picked on by an older boy at school. With my friends being occupied, I try and look elsewhere to avoid him mentally, and I notice the students from my former school.

Meanwhile, her boyfriend continues to put on this act and all of the sudden it seems like all eyes are on us. I am ready just to turn around and head straight for the exit and leave everybody here. He becomes the final straw as he smiles towards the ex-girlfriend, gives her a head nod, and then turns to me and says "We know she made the right choice." He just gave me all the reason to throw care out of the window, and I explode. I completely lose control and become hostile by using vulgar language towards him as loud as I can. This attracted eyes from everyone including my friends, his friends, the ex-girlfriend, old classmates, and complete strangers. The ex-girlfriend pulls me away, and she slaps me across the face.

I don't say anything, let them all walk away together and tell my friends I am not sticking around here anymore. We were there for less than an hour when the whole ordeal occurs and now the night has become an entire waste. I am sure some people enjoyed the show, but I know for my friends it meant embarrassment, putting them in a tight spot, and almost forcing their hand at leaving the festival. They could have stayed, and I would have walked home by myself. But, because of me they left and their night of fun ended as well.

Another week goes by, and I receive a call out of nowhere from one of the old basketball teammates. He invites me over to his house for a party he is having over the weekend. For a brief moment, he talks about all the people that will be there and how great it would be to hang out. I think he can tell I'm on the fence about attending. After what happened at the festival I have no intention of going through another night like that. A little hesitation only lasted for a short while, and I make the decision to go. Besides, if anything I can always sneak in alcohol to deal with it.

As soon as we get to the house I hide the water bottle in my back pocket. The doorbell rings and his parents come to the door. A feeling of guilt sets right in my stomach. His parents look up to me as a good, well-rounded, and responsible friend. I remember them sitting in the stands at our basketball games and having his dad coach me in some of the earlier years. They were proud of my success in basketball, and I always felt they were happy to see it because of what I went through with the diabetes ordeal when it happened.

I put on a fake smile and head downstairs to the basement where I meet up with the old teammate. We talk briefly, but as soon as we started it ended because he had to make his way around to all the others. There are people here from four different high schools, and I can put maybe a fourth of the names to people's faces. I feel uncomfortable already, and I don't want to be here. Feelings of anxiousness and being out of place begin to sink in. Thinking about everything going on I realize what is in my hands, sitting there in my lap. Directly in the line of sight is the water bottle full of vodka. There is no hesitation and within a few moments the bottle is empty.

Moments later I am lying on the floor with two cushions. My old teammate's younger sister comes down to see that I am lying still on the cushions. She looks at me and wonders what's wrong. His father comes down, and he covers up for me explaining that I am not feeling good. The younger sister looks at me and says, "Is he sick?" What a disappointing feeling his father must have towards me at this point.

I am sick. I feel disgusting and dirty. Feelings that I, unfortunately, have become all too familiar with. Sick of so many things to a point where it becomes easier to recognize all the misery in life and lack an inability to notice anything going right. I am sick of having to deal with all of the maintenance and dread of living with a disease that I cannot control. I am tired of going to school and wanting nothing more but the day to be over so I can leave. I am sick of being uncomfortable around peers my age, in the same school, and even in the same classes. I am even tired of drinking.

I don't know how long I have been sitting here thinking about all this. Maybe it was enough time for the alcohol to wear off a little, and I get the urge to get up and head outside. Everyone else is still downstairs, and his family is occupying the rest of the house. I grab a basketball inside his garage and start shooting in his driveway. If I would've just made the basketball team freshman year this would all be different. Life wouldn't be like this if that one thing could have happened.

A friend comes through the garage door and approaches me outside. He doesn't say anything and for a while only stands there. It is clear he is searching for something, anything to say to get me to snap out of all of this. I get a sense he would grab me and just shake me back and forth if he felt it would work. But, I get the feeling he sees that I am struggling more than he can solve. I see a look that acknowledges this pain I am fighting through but not having any answer to help get me past it. And to a friend, that must be incredibly difficult to go through.

I start to realize the only result of my drinking is making everything else worse. I used to think alcohol stopped my compulsive thinking, but it only makes it worse shortly after. I don't realize it at this point because my mind is too altered, and I am too depressed to tell myself that drinking is destroying me instead of helping. One of the primary reasons for drinking is to hide and avoid my feelings and emotions concerning my diabetes. Alcohol makes the conditions of my diabetes worse. I can feel it in me that my conditions are worsening. The physical symptoms are putting me through even more misery. When I am trying to hide the emotional pain of diabetes, I am making the physical pain even worse. Then when the physical pain starts, it has an effect on my emotional and mental status.

I want to believe desperately that drinking is going to help get me through this. Where does that sound familiar? How long have I been desperately hoping that neglecting my diabetes would somehow get me through it? I continue to believe that drinking will stop me from being depressed and lonely. Once again, the drinking contradicts its initial purpose. I feel even more desolate while I am drinking. I continue to believe that neglecting my diabetes will help me feel less of a diabetic. If I don't take my blood sugar levels on insulin injections than it would help me avoid thinking about it. But, when the adverse and harmful effects of the poorly managed diabetes kicks in than it is right there for me.

Something inside me knows that all of this is not working, and yet nothing is telling me to stop doing it. Instead of being miserable I figure it will be better to be drunk and miserable. I began drinking to celebrate what could hopefully be the beginning of something new. And after that failed I continued to drink to escape unwanted thoughts and feelings associated with the personal troubles in my life. Neglecting my diabetes in these moments provides some relief by not having to poke my fingers, stab myself with needles, count the food I have to eat, and document everything. The drinking, forgetting about school responsibilities, and neglectful approach to diabetes provided short term comfort in those moments where I struggled most in what life. I only wanted to get through all those moments, whether in a good way or bad way, and just make it through the end of the day.

This is the way coping, or lack of, worked for me. In a sense, it does work. In those moments where health, school, and social life become miserable those actions led to only getting through the misery. But it would quickly result in more pain in which the only way I knew how to get through it was by the very same actions. At least it got me through that until it lead me straight into another destructive behavior. I don't know what else to do at this point. I have been dishonest to everyone ranging from my parents, friends, peers, doctors, nurses, and teachers. How can I ask for help on all these issues when all I have been doing is manipulating, lying, hiding, avoiding, and escaping everything?

I know my method isn't working because at the end of the day I am not finding any brighter horizons. Day after day, the lack of wanting anything but a cure for my chronic illness left me believing there was nothing out there for me that would be worthwhile until that cure was there. I deserve it too. Everything about that day was unfair and completely out of my control. To have something come out of nowhere and take everything away from me leaves no justification whatsoever.

Until something else decides to come along and give everything back, I do not see any other ways to deal with my life struggles. Being comfortable in misery is not something I planned on using as a means of dealing with it all. I see having type one diabetes as nothing but misery. What good has ever come out of it? How has this disease benefited me in any way whatsoever since entering my life?

Plus, it's a misery that no one I know understands, and there's no way I am close enough to begin opening those doors. So I might as well let other misery sink in that other people can actually relate to. Problems at school, ex-girlfriend, and social issues are more identifiable. Not only identifiable, but those problems have solutions. But living a life with diabetes, there are no answers. Hopefully, the focus will stay on top while the actual pain is kept in the darkness.

CHAPTER 10

Contemplating My Existence

"To contemplate is to look at shadows."

Quote Inspired by Victor Hugo

The out of control drinking on the weekends and depressing weekdays creates a powerful combination to crash head on with the insecurities surrounding my diabetes. About three or four weeks before my sophomore year of school ends I start to have even stronger feelings of anger, sadness, and hatred towards my diabetes. I sit in class all day thinking about it to the point where everything around me becomes almost nonexistent. Not because they aren't necessarily saying anything to me, but mentally I become so checked out that it's like I'm not there.

I'm still struggling with the simple, fundamental fact of having this disease. Even after nearly four years of being diagnosed with this chronic illness I continue to have a hard time with the disease itself. The truth that I am a type one diabetic and have to live with it potentially for the rest of my life destroys me inside. It drives me crazy that no one; not even specialists, can explain the reason for developing the disease. The realization and fact that I have diabetes becomes depressing to me. My compulsive thoughts are rapidly going through my mind: *Why do I have diabetes? Am I going to live with this forever? What did I do to deserve this? Will there ever be a cure?*

Even when I try and get beyond all the questions, I sit here and ask myself, "*What do I do now with my diabetes?*" I don't have any family or friends who have this disease. Immediately I feel different than everyone else because of my disease since I was diagnosed. There is no family member or a close friend whom I can consult with or relate to when it comes to issues surrounding my diabetes. I feel different, and I feel disgusting. It's been hard enough for my family having to deal with everything since the hospital nightmare, the doctor's appointments afterward, the financial concerns, the sleepless nights, and the whole transferring schools ordeal. Last thing I want to do is burden them more.

Being an adolescent, it is hard to cope with my diabetes because I don't have any friends living with it. I feel uncomfortable seeking guidance from them because no one has the disease. Not only am I uncomfortable seeking advice, but I feel different than all my friends in a negative way. Even though my friends never say or gesture in any way that I am looked at as different, that's how I feel. Diabetes leaves me feeling all alone and different than everyone else that I knew. That's why it's easier to let other issues take the spotlight. My friends can relate more to someone struggling in classes or dealing with a former girlfriend.

The maintenance of diabetes is something I have never been able to manage on my own. And yet, as I get older I keep pushing everyone away and claim to be responsible enough to take care of myself. Since the diagnosis, I had doctors, nurses, and my parents around the clock taking care of the condition and telling me what to do. Even when I transitioned home after spending a week in the hospital, I had a nurse stop by regularly to see how I was doing. Now, I keep saying to myself that this is my problem and my life, and I can do everything on my own.

Truth be told, living with diabetes is a lot of hard work. This disease requires attention multiple times, every single day. Every day it's about eating right, taking my blood four times a day, measuring insulin, taking injections, and getting the right amount of exercise. It never ends, and as far as I know the treatment and maintenance will never end. How exciting is that? No days off, no vacation from it, only a constant daily reminder of having a chronic illness. The only breaks I receive are the times when I neglect to take care of it, and even then those are short lived as the consequences of ill health quickly follow.

Being a type one diabetic, the goal for the average blood glucose is to be between seventy and a hundred and twenty. My blood glucose level was at fourteen hundred when I was initially diagnosed. Numbers below seventy and levels above one hundred and twenty are potentially harmful and pose a risk. There is a lot of room for error. Life with diabetes and managing blood glucose levels is like walking a tightrope.

Feels like I already have more room for failure than I do at success. More chances to mess up than to do the right thing. And to be quite frank, I became exquisite at failing, messing up and not doing the right thing. Not taking my blood sugar levels, refusing to do insulin injections, not counting the carbohydrates, and eating unhealthy foods became a lot more inconvenient than thinking about having to do all of these tasks multiple times throughout the day. I never got into a routine of handling all this on top of everything else life is made up of. But, the day I was diagnosed with diabetes it was difficult to see anything past that.

Living with type one diabetes does not leave a lot of room for error. As I walk my tightrope, something may cause my blood glucose level to go up or down the healthy level. It goes up a little, and I begin to fall off the tightrope. It goes down a little bit and I begin to fall off the tightrope. Back and forth, back and forth, back and forth. Living with diabetes is steadily walking this thin line that doesn't appear to get any thicker. The safety net is nowhere near. If I fall, or when I fall, I will more than likely end up being left with a painful health condition.

Most people never take their blood glucose levels. They live their lives and eat sweets, consume carbohydrates, and never stop to think of what their body is doing. Most people have the ability to control their levels without having to do much work. Their bodies produce insulin and regulate the glucose levels by itself. When an individual is diagnosed with diabetes, they are the ones who have to do the work. Our bodies don't have the luxury of being able to stay in the healthy blood glucose range. The main way we do is by drawing up the insulin from a vial into a syringe and having to inject it into ourselves.

Both low and high blood glucose levels never feel pleasant. Low glucose levels make you feel dizzy, weak, and very irritated. The dizziness and weakness can be overcome by consuming sugar. When I feel my blood glucose is low, I can eat everything in the house. There are times when the level feels so low that I eat half a cake. I know if I am to drink some juice or have half a peanut butter sandwich the level will go back up to normal. As soon as I eat half a sandwich I am still hungry, and the only way to speed up the process is it eat more. High blood glucose levels create increase urination and extreme thirst.

One of the misconceptions I hear about diabetes is a person gets used to the treatment and maintenance. Out of all the finger pokes and insulin injections, it would be nice to think at some point my body would adjust or deal with it better. It would be such a sigh of relief knowing that the small poke in the fingers will feel like a soft cushion on impact. Or it would be even more relieving to know that a syringe will feel like it's going into a piece of fruit; just like how I used to have to practice in the hospital when I was first diagnosed.

But, you never get used to the physical feeling of finger pokes and insulin injections. Each time there is worry that the needles will cause physical pain and discomfort. And each time this brings about feelings of stress and anxiety. There are times when everything goes entirely well without feeling any pain whatsoever. On the other hand, there are times when the needle hurts more than anything. One of the toughest parts is not knowing what the experience is going to be like and being stuck with nothing but the thoughts of doubt.

For the first four years of living with diabetes, I take an average of four insulin injections a day. Four injections multiplied by 365 days equals 1,460 injections in a single year. 1,460 injections per year for four years equal 5,840 injections. Personally, I do not know what amount is considered to be a lot and what is considered a little. All I know is that 1,460 injections a year is a lot. Some people say they can't stand having to get an injection once or twice in a single year, let alone four times in a single day. Insulin injections hurt more than they feel good. Having to treat continuously and maintain diabetes feeds into my anger and hate.

The only thing worse than the physical discomfort is the emotional turmoil. The hospitals, the doctors, and treatment workers are great at providing me with help when it comes to the physical treatment of diabetes. However, I never receive the emotional support I need for coping with my disease. No one guides me to learning how to co-exist with diabetes and still live a happy life with this chronic illness. Without receiving treatment for the emotional pain inside of me, the thoughts and feelings continue to grow in the direction of anger and hatred.

There are also many common myths about type one diabetes that creates confusion and frustration. Whenever people talk about it or discuss the disease, they would usually discuss the sugar aspects of it and other misconceptions. People say insulin cures diabetes. If only that were true. If only there were a cure that I could take that would rid me of this terrible illness. But there isn't, and insulin is surely not a cure. Taking insulin keeps me alive on a daily basis, but does not cure the disease. There is no cure for diabetes. Nor does insulin prevent the development of complications, which can include kidney failure, blindness, amputation, heart attack, stroke, and nerve damage.

People say I can never eat sweets. People think I can't enjoy chocolate, cakes, fresh baked cookies, muffins, frosted cupcakes, candy, or any other dessert. People tell me I can't eat anything with sugar. Limiting sweets will help people with type one diabetes keep their blood levels under control by requiring less insulin to be administered; but that does not mean sugar cannot be consumed. And, if the blood level drops too low, sweets must be consumed to raise it, and prevent the onset of hypoglycemia.

All of these reasons; having the disease, feeling alone and different, having to continuously treat and maintain the disease, and the emotional pain, along with the common myths I always hear about, do nothing more than add fuel to the angry fire of hate deep down inside. I find myself thinking more and more about my health on a daily basis. It becomes more frustrating and irritating to where I neglect my diabetes maintenance quite regularly.

School becomes a blur, the issue with the ex-girlfriend becomes obsolete, the drinking and social problems become a waste, and yet diabetes always remains right there. When everything was going well and then completely changed, the only thing to remain the same and consistent was the diabetes. It feels like it constantly wants to remind me of that during times when I least want to deal with it. At times where I just want to turn around and walk away from the misery diabetes greets me right there.

I hate diabetes more than anything. Picturing having to live with this disease for the rest of my life tears me up inside. I am still mistreating my health by rarely taking my blood and not always taking the correct amount of insulin. Sometimes when I inject insulin onto my arms or legs, a small quantity of the insulin is blocked and comes out. My arms have bruises, yellow and dark marks where the syringe has inflicted pain.

Most importantly, I hate diabetes because I have a fear one day it will kill me. I am afraid of my diabetes, and it has become an enemy of whom I which to avoid coming into conflict with. Life as a diabetic is going to be a continuous fight until I am finally dead. It almost killed me once, and it is something people say was entirely out of anyone's control. So what do I do if it decides to do it again in which I have no control over what diabetes can do to me?

The struggle deep down inside is too much for me, and I want to end all the pain in any way that I can. My initial suicide thoughts occurred when I was recovering in the hospital after my near-death experience. At first, I thought killing myself would stop any future complications and pain that I may experience because of my diabetes. I also thought that being diabetic would be a burden to my family. Diabetes would be an emotional and financial struggle for them; a battle that wouldn't be easy. Killing myself would take away that battle and I would no longer be a burden to them.

I go to school, and nothing changes. I continue to struggle in classes and make no attempt to achieve in any academics. Walking through the halls and trying to converse with classmates continues to be uncomfortable. Taking care of my diabetes is a rare occurrence and neglecting my health is normal. I only want to see the rare good friends and go home at the end of the day as soon as possible. I stay up all night thinking about everything going on. My eyes finally get heavy, and I fall asleep.

All of the sudden I open my eyes and I am lying down in an ambulance, looking through the windows. Through the small window, I can see the hospital sitting on top of the hill. My head is spinning, and my vision turns pitch black and I am unconscious. I wake up again and this time three or four nurses are poking me with medical tools and talking about me in a language I do not understand. All of the sudden my vision turns black and when it comes back the nurse is puncturing me stomach with a syringe, and I scream.

The scream is in my head, and I wake up from the nightmare. The nightmares are occurring again, and this time, more often and more vivid. The memories of what happened to me are being played over and over again in my mind. I want the nightmares and flashbacks to stop. I hate them, and it only adds fuel to the anger and growing hate for diabetes. I don't want to sleep anymore, so I stay up and sleep very little.

The initial suicide thoughts enter my mind again. This time they are twice as powerful. My first thoughts are occurring at a time when I wasn't facing these difficult situations. I wasn't having school problems, wasn't having social anxiety, wasn't drinking alcohol on the weekends and wasn't having relationship issues. Now that I am going through all these personal troubles, and my hatred for diabetes is growing stronger it makes sense in my head suicide will end all the pain and misery.

I start to think suicide will be beneficial to me. Even though it will cause my family and friends a lot of pain, I think in the long run it will eventually bring them a sense of relief. Since the diagnosis, I always felt like a burden to my family and friends. There is guilt inside of me for the burden I have placed on them. With me being dead, I feel it's the only way I could attempt to wipe the slate clean of everything diabetes has done to others.

The primary benefit of committing suicide is the relief of no longer having to ever deal with diabetes every again. If I kill myself, I will no longer have diabetes. To me, suicide is the only potential cure available. This will mean no more blood meters, finger pokes, insulin shots, carbohydrate counting, low blood sugars, high blood sugars, and doctor appointments. Diabetes continues to inflict pain, and I want to end it all.

I never seek out treatment for the suicidal thoughts. The school year is coming to a closure, and I want it to end more than anything. It's been a year of struggling with going to school and even transferring here. I go to school every morning with this flat, depressing, emotionless expression on my face. I sit at my locker before classes staring ahead, drifting once again into the dark maze in my head. Finding reasons to go to school and make it through the day seem more and more difficult.

Trying to sort through my thoughts, feelings, and emotions are like an attempt to find a needle in a haystack the size of an amusement park. I am searching for a reason behind everything. I still can't believe this is happening to me. I grew up with two loving parents who did everything they could to love, care, and help me find happiness. I have close friends who care and watch over me. My battle isn't with the outside world though. The battle exists in my world; the maze I have been lost and trapped in for almost four years now.

Even though I am uncomfortable discussing my thoughts and feelings with people whom can get me the professional help I need, I do continue to talk to close friends. They know about the drinking and take care of me when I decide drinking is necessary. Some people know more than others, but no one knows about the dreadful view of my diabetes. Everyone seems to take the bait, believing the depression, social anxiety, and drinking is because of the conflict with the ex-girlfriend and getting adjusted to a new school.

I don't go home to drink on the weekends because of her; I do it because I am trying to stop my compulsive thinking and deal with my emotions and feelings. I am not having social anxiety because of the ex-girlfriend and classmates; it is because of the insecurities of diabetes. I don't struggle academically because of her; I don't have any motivation and can barely concentrate on anything because of what is going on inside my head. I don't contemplate suicide because of her; I do it because I hate diabetes. It is my cure for the disease, and I feel I am lifting a burden off of my family and friends.

Despite the benefit of not having to deal with insecurities and issues, I am feeling guilty for hiding bits and pieces of the truth from friends. It doesn't feel good, not for one minute, to let the whole ordeal be placated to prevent them from helping me out. The secrecy is making me feel less of a friend than I want to be. But, I'm not ready to talk about anything related to my diabetes because to me there is no end in sight.

I wake up in the middle of the night after having another nightmare, and I am filled with anger and hate. I can't stand the nightmares anymore, and the flashbacks are dating back to the day I was diagnosed. There is a burning sensation inside of me that wants to end the pain. I sit at the end of the bed and think hard about finding any reason or rationale to keep me from wanting to give up. I stare at the floor and remember my mother having to sit there for nights on end when I returned from the hospital. I look over to the window and remember seeing her in the hospital window crying when I finally came to after being treated.

Sleeping is no longer an option, and now I am up in the middle of the night with panic, anxiety, worry, and frustration building inside. I pace around my room frantically, but the frustration and anger remains. I hate everything about life. I hate diabetes. I hate all the maintenance that carries so much physical and emotional pain. I hate what happened at my old school. I hate what's going on at this school. I hate the fact that I feel different. I hate feeling lost, feeling disgusting, and feeling like I have no place of belonging. The hate is growing so strong am I can't take it anymore.

I think about going downstairs and running on the treadmill. As I make my way out of my room and down the stairs, I get the idea of wanting others to hate the diabetes as much as me. Maybe if they hated diabetes as much as me, it would justify all the misery I have created. Before heading down the basement stairs, I pass the cabinet that holds all of my diabetes supplies. I stop there a moment and just freeze. My eyes glare over all the insulin bottles, packs of syringes, finger pokes, boxes of meds, and booklets full of information. I hate all of it.

Thinking about running on the treadmill and seeing all the diabetic supplies puts together the dangerous idea of being able to end it all and have everyone hate it as much as I do. I open up the kit and draw up thirty units of insulin. I say this is it in my head and stab myself with the insulin injection. The amount of insulin, not consuming sugar, and exercising are the components that will send my blood sugar level crashing to absolute nothing. I put on my running shoes that I brought down with me and head downstairs. My father is out of town on business, so his office is empty. There is no way I would attempt to do this while he was right there working.

I think about the hate, and all I want to do is end the pain. I begin to run on the treadmill. I increase the rate of speed faster and faster. My legs are burning already. They are burning with the fire and hate in my life, and I want everything to end. If I keep this up, I will drive my blood sugar down to zero, and that will kill me. If I die this way, nobody will ever know about the insecurities about diabetes. They will be left with the false idea that I am trying to take care of my health by exercising. They will think I went downstairs to work out and use exercise as a source of controlling my blood levels. Everyone will hate diabetes. They will think it killed me and will begin to feel the hate I have been experiencing for all these years.

I run on the treadmill and think at any moment I will feel dizzy enough and pass out from my blood level dropping so low. As strange as it sounds it starts to feel comforting. The idea of this being the last shot and no more insulin injections is relieving. No more finger pokes. No more appointments at the hospitals. No more sleepless nights because of nightmares or flashbacks. No more social isolation because of insecurities. No more causing my family and friends any more pain than I already have. No more misery.

All of the sudden I look up and see a picture on the nearest corner of my father's desk. I see my father and the three of us siblings standing in front of a famous landmark attraction. The train station sits atop the entrance to Walt Disney World's Magic Kingdom. We are smiling, and my mom is the one taking the picture. A flood of cherished memories enters my mind and heart as my running begins to slow down. The more I think about the love and the happiness with my family the less I think about the pain of diabetes.

The picture makes me think about my family. I think about mom. I think about dad. I think about my sister. I think about my brother. My mind, with all of the hate and pain going on inside, finally slows down and right there focuses on my family. I see their faces. I see their smiles. Most importantly, I see the smile on my face. A time when happiness was never hard to find, and the misery was something entirely obsolete. Even at such a young age I remember wanting more and more out of life. Wanting to dream, wanting to be creative, and wanting to be something more than just ordinary.

I can't do it. I can't kill myself. I can't put them through the pain of losing somebody they love. I immediately turn the treadmill off and head upstairs to the kitchen. My hands are shaking, and I open the cabinets and grab a bowl, a cereal box, and the gallon of milk. I sit at the kitchen table and eat a bowl of cereal. Tears begin to fill up in my eyes, and I can't stop crying. I eat, and I cry. I eat, and I cry. I am done with one bowl, and I begin eating a second. I am weak. I am weak because I don't even have the strength to kill myself. I am weak because I don't even have the strength to overcome the suicidal thoughts in my head. I eat a third bowl and a fourth. I eat enough to the point where my blood sugar is high.

I head upstairs and get ready. I see my mom getting ready for work and my brother getting ready for school. No words are exchanged, and I don't give them any clue of what I just tried to do. I drive to school, get out of the car and walk towards school. It is another average day. Students are carrying out the usual routine of heading to school and making their way to their lockers. As soon as I walk through the doors a student hands me a yellow ribbon and yellow card that is for suicide prevention. Right there and then I am given the help I need. I think in my head again. *What do I do? Should I call it?*

I feel too embarrassed about the whole situation, so I secretly slip the ribbon and card in my pocket. *What would other students think if I were to call the suicide number? What would my close friends think? What would my family think?* I don't have the strength to seek help.

As soon as I make my way down the hall to the lockers a friend of mine noticed I am wearing a yellow shirt that just so happens to be the same resemblance as the suicide prevention color. Even though it is purely a coincidence, I can't believe I am wearing the same color. Already, as I felt before, the day is beginning to be a nightmare. I am uncomfortable, and I am uneasy.

Shortly afterward, the ex-girlfriend stops by and strikes up a conversation about how I have been acting. I don't want to deal with her at all right now and within minutes we get into a verbal argument. She leaves, and before heading to class, I say to some friends standing around, "I really can't take any more of this." I head off without saying anything else.

But that does not work either. After a couple of minutes of being in class, a student stops by and notifies the teacher that I am being summoned to the guidance counselor's office. As I head down to her office, I am thinking she is calling me in to talk about something with transferring or something of little importance. To my surprise, the guidance counselor cuts right to the chase and explains that another guidance counselor notified her of my well-being after two of his students expressed their concerns.

As soon as she tells me about the incident I immediately feel betrayed by whomever it is that talked to the guidance counselor. *Who the hell told them about me? What did they tell them? Why didn't they tell me?* As these thoughts circulate in my head, she explains my mother is coming to pick me up, and I am excused from school for the rest of the day. I don't want to see my mom at this point, but at the same time I do. My father and mother have always done whatever humanly possible in their power to take care of me and love me, especially during the struggle with my diabetes. I don't want to see her because of all the pain I know I have caused.

I have no idea what I am going to say to her. She pulls up, I sit in the car, and right away I can feel the tension in the air. It is the most uncomfortable moment in my life with her. The relationship with my parents has always been excellent. There is never any fighting, and I am not afraid to share my life with them. And then diabetes had to change everything. I lie to them about blood levels and lie to them about neglecting my health. I keep the secrets of my dark depression and struggle to co-exist with my diabetes. The atmosphere is quiet as a tomb on the drive home.

As we pull into the neighborhood, my mom turns to me and says, "A.J., do you want to live?" What a horrible question a mother must feel she has to ask her son. I feel so ashamed that she has to push herself to ask. What a great son I turned out to be. At this moment, nothing has changed about my hatred for my diabetes, the depression, the social anxiety, and the academic struggles. Something did change, however.

As the silence grows, I remember looking at the picture of my family in Walt Disney World. I remember thinking about all my family, relatives, and close friends that mean everything to me. I found something to hold on to and fight for. I look into my mother's eyes and say, "Yes I do, and I am going to fix this." At this moment my suicidal thoughts vanish, and I know right now it is no longer an option. They haven't escaped, but for now they are out of my sight and have been consumed by the darkness. I still hate my life, but I found what I need to fight and stay alive for; my family.

If I am not going to do it for myself, I will do it for them. At first, I thought suicide will help my family and friends. I feel I am a burden to everyone and killing myself will take that burden away. However as I looked into my mother's eyes, I saw the desperation and pain she was almost preparing for if my answer would have been no. Committing suicide will create an immense amount of pain for them as well. I picture what life will be like if I kill myself. I try stepping into the shoes of my family and friends and see what it would look like if a close friend or family killed themselves. It only takes a short time for me to see what I would have caused, and I can't go through with it.

Through a mutual agreement my mother and I decide it would be best to go see a psychologist to help address the issues at hand. The psychologist is a complete stranger, and there's no way I am ready to share the dark secrets and pain hidden inside. So, I manipulate the session by focusing on what is clear. The only problems that I want to discuss with him are those associated with school, the ex-girlfriend, and some of the social anxiety.

"Let's do a little exercise shall we?" He insists. "Imagine your life. Everything that has happened in your past, in the present time, and what lies ahead of you in the future. Think deep. Relax. Now, imagine your life portrayed as a road. Can you do that?"

"Yes," I reply.

"Good. Keep thinking. Your life portrayed as a road. Now, take a deep breath and describe it to me."

I take a deep breath in, hold it, and exhale deeply. And I begin. "It was once a beautiful road. The road was pure black with that sharp asphalt look to it. The center line is freshly painted. The road is smooth and safe. Safe to drive on. Safe to walk on. Safe to be traveling on."

Another deep breath and I continue. "It is damaged now. Pebbles are scattered across the road, and cracks are tearing it up. The black asphalt is now gray and faded. The center line that was a boundary is worn off completely. The road is damaged. Destructive and abusive tracks have made its way through, ripping the shreds out of the once safe road. The road is damaged and looks miserable."

The psychologist stops me and asks, "What is on the side of the road? Grass? Hills? Trees?"

"Nothing but dirt," I respond. "Just like in an old western. Nothing but flat land covered in dry dirt. A couple of shrubs here and there and tumbleweeds scatter across the ground once in a while."

"What's in front of you? What lies ahead?" He asks.

"Darkness. It is pitch black. I can't see past the darkness. Storm clouds settle in, but there is no rain, no lightning. Everything is surrounded in pure darkness."

"Look behind you, in the opposite direction," He instructs. "What do you see back there?"

I try and think of what is behind me, and nothing is there. I try harder and think deeper, but still nothing. "Nothing's there," I say.

"What do you mean?" he asks.

"There is nothing behind me. It's white, like an empty page in an artist's sketchpad."

Our time is up, and I leave the office. I get in my car and head home. I think about the exercise and most importantly, the blank page behind me. *Why is there nothing behind me? Why can't I see a beautiful road that once was? Am I destined to walk the path leading to complete darkness? Is it a symbol that I can't live my old life again?*

My road is a transformed symbol of the dark maze my mind continues to be trapped in. The road symbolizes all the destructive and negative areas in my life; the diabetes, the depression, the drinking, the school troubles, the relationship issues, the suicide thoughts, the social anxiety, and all the pain that goes along with them. Not only do I feel trapped in a maze I can't escape, but now I feel lost walking down this lonely, dark road. The maze becomes even more clustered with the destructive behaviors and compulsive thoughts going through my mind.

The psychologist helps me identify thoughts and feelings to my presenting troubles. Most of my counseling time is spent talking about the transition from schools. Probably because the whole referral began with the issues occurring there. I have a lot of guilt and feelings of sadness over the decision to leave my former school. Maybe not the decision to leave, but how I decided to leave. Inside I still feel I betrayed the only good friends I did have when I left.

"How do you feel about your decision to transfer schools?" He asks.

"Had to be done," I respond.

"Are you sure?"

"Things weren't working out. Grades were terrible. Wasn't making any friends. Had to be done."

"Do you still talk to some people from there?"

"A few," I say. "But not as much as I should."

"What about the people you don't talk to?"

"What about them?" I respond hastily.

"Can I ask you a question?"

A question with a question. A regular occurrence in my counseling sessions with him. What if I said no? Think he would simply accept and move forward? "Go ahead."

"How come you didn't reach out more to some of the real close people you had? I mean your sister and cousin were at the one school, and now you have your brother and close neighborhood brother at this school."

This strikes a chord. I still feel guilty for leaving the school because of my cousin. We have been like brothers since we were little kids. I just up and left without making any attempt to talk to him about what was going on and what is still going on for that matter. Even though my sister graduated already it became clear in my head that I failed to reach out to her when we were attending the same school together. My brother reached out more than I ever have for him. And I didn't have the courage to talk even to a neighborhood

103

brother. I start to create a bunch of excuses and justifications in my head. Only this time my heart decides to speak instead.

"That's what living with a chronic condition can do to you. Makes you feel lonelier than you can ever imagine." I had to stop for a minute as my emotions are beginning to build up. He tells me to take a few deep breaths and continue when I am ready.

"You…" I begin. But I stop as the trembling gets worse. "You don't listen to anyone, even when they are talking to you. You don't see anyone, even when they are staring right at you. And you feel all by yourself, even when people who love you are standing right beside you."

I just sit in here in silence. I look to see if he is talking in case my mind has drifted away from our conversation. But he doesn't say anything, and I continue to sit there for a few minutes. Our time is up, and I go home.

The end of the school year is not over yet. The past couple of weeks feels more like a couple of months. My counseling sessions are helping, but there are still a lot of unresolved issues. One night a good friend, the car guy, calls me and starts discussing some of the personal struggles he is facing. We decide to drive around for a while to reminisce over our troubled minds. Driving around becomes our method for releasing our thoughts and feelings, just like going to Starbucks is for the sarcastic guy and myself.

While driving around he wants to take me to a place where he goes to clear his mind. He pulls off into a series of office buildings, over a small bridge, and parks in one of the parking lots. He gets out of the car and starts making his way to his known destination. We make our way back to the bridge we had driven over. Instead of walking across the bridge, he leads me below into this place of ease, comfort, and relaxation. Below the bridge is a man-made pond surrounded by a large cluster of rocks.

We sit down and start talking about what is going on in our lives. For one of the first times in my life I begin to open up to what is really going on inside my head. Without fear, without hesitation, without a doubt, and without concern about how he will react. He's not going through what I'm going through, but he takes the time to listen to whatever I have to say. The conversations start simple, and the discussions continue to grow from there. I still don't see any solutions to what is going on, but at least this is feeling like a start to something different.

CHAPTER 11

Sick and Tired

"Only when you are sick of being
sick can you be cured."

Quote Inspired by Lao Tzu, author of *Tao Te Ching*

"Do you know what we should do?" The car guy asks as he skips a rock across the water.

"What's that?"

"We need to get out of here for a while."

"Are you serious?"

"Yeah. Just out of here for a while to get away from all of this."

"Where would we go?"

"I don't know. Somewhere away from here though."

I think about his idea. Maybe he's right. Maybe I just need to get out of town for a while to break free from everything that has gone on. I think about everything going on with my diabetes, school, the social anxiety, and the depression. I think about leaving, and it brings about a sense of relief that maybe I could momentarily leave everything behind and get a chance to catch up with my thoughts.

I return home and head downstairs to do some work with my dad. It's another simple envelope project of sending out a couple hundred mailings to people and places. As I fill the envelopes, close them, and label them I think about my father. I don't know what his thoughts are regarding what happened at school and seeing a psychologist. I turn to him and explain that I need to get away for the weekend. After some questioning and investigating he understands the desire to leave.

He makes the proper arrangements and this upcoming weekend the three of us, including the car guy, are going to go to Wisconsin Dells. On the car ride up we are all listening to our separate music.

"What are you listening to?" I ask.

"Thinking music," he responds.

"Good old thinking music," I say. Brings a little smile to my face. Thinking that something I started has been passed from friend to friend.

This trip to the Dells isn't meant to be a time to go have fun and forget about the troubles I am facing. In fact, on the drive up there I decide I want this weekend to be the time for me to think carefully about what is going on and try to understand where my life is heading. This opportunity gives me a chance to think about everything without the high number of distractions from back home. I don't want to stay in the dark maze, being lost and lonely, nor do I wish to travel down the dark and depressing road. But, no matter how hard I try looking past it the only scene ahead is darkness, and this is the only direction I can see my life going.

We decide only to tell a small, select number of people we are leaving. Our parents both know and the only other person that is aware of our plan is the sarcastic guy. I planned on telling him from the very beginning about our idea to leave. It is surprising to hear him say this is a good idea, and it can have a lot of potentials to benefit the emotional struggle inside of me. Inside I feel guilty for not telling some of the others. But at this point I trust these two the most.

I spend the majority of my time listening to music, writing, and spending it with my father and friend. It's nice to get away and feel

107

like problems are far away. It was helpful to my friend as well; as he was able to get some time to think and process some of the issues he was facing. As far as my dad goes, I have this feeling it is reassuring and welcoming just to get to spend time with me after everything that has occurred. He doesn't say it, but I get the sense he would say the getaway was rewarding as well.

Finally, my sophomore year comes to a bitter end. The year was filled with so many painful and personal struggles that continue to be unresolved. Everything I try fixing or changing ends up getting worse. I transferred to a school where I continue to perform negatively in my academic studies, and my insecurities continue to prevent me from making more friends. I attempted to fix everything between the ex-girlfriend and me which ends up making it worse than it ever was. The depression was supposed to go away and disappear when my life at a new school started. Instead, everything that was supposed to get better becomes worse. Not only does everything get worse, but I develop new issues with my alcohol use and suicidal thoughts.

The "World's Largest Musical Festival," known as Summerfest is now taking place. It's tradition here in Milwaukee, and I do make my way down there on a couple of occasions. One occasion I decide to drink before we head down there. My friend drives my car to the nearest park and ride. Before we leave, I fill an empty water bottle full of vodka. You can usually get away with sneaking alcohol into the Summerfest grounds, but I don't need to.

I consume the whole water bottle of vodka, straight up, in the time it takes us to get from my house to the park and ride. I look over at my fiend and when he notices the water bottle full of vodka is already polished off I can clearly see he is not impressed whatsoever. It is obvious that my friends want me to stop drinking. They make that loud and clear from the very beginning. I wonder if they are afraid to say something because then I would most likely consume alcohol alone, and the idea of that probably scares them more.

The counseling sessions and time with good friends helps make the compulsive thoughts slow down a little bit. But, as soon as I begin to drink alcohol the fast paced thoughts about all the misery quickly surfaces. I start to think of not having fun, seeing people I don't want to see, feeling uncomfortable around others, and not caring about the impact on my diabetes. The more alcohol I consume, the more the self-destructive thoughts take over.

Shortly after arriving, and being under the influence, I tell my friend I want to go home already. For some reason, he doesn't hesitate or try and convince me to stay. Maybe he feels it will be best for me to go home because staying out drinking would likely cause more destruction. He takes me back, and I call another friend, the sweetheart and talk to her about what happened. I tell her about drinking and wanting to leave right away because of what was starting to go through my mind.

When I tell her about the drinking at Summerfest she becomes disappointed, however, she is more upset and worried about what I am doing to my health. I put her, as with all my friends, through a lot of fear and wrong places. They are all concerned about my destructive behaviors and overall well-being. The main concern for them is the physical health of my diabetes, which I have to say, is still not a concern for me. However, the worry and concern I continue to cause my family and friends makes me feel guilty for what I have done and continue to do repeatedly like clockwork. She reminds me to check my blood before getting off the phone and going to bed.

July is approaching, and my father tells me about a series of trips to Illinois he is going to be making throughout the whole month. He invites me to be gone seventeen out of the thirty-one days. I am hesitant at first to go on the trips, but after some consideration and advice I decide to go. Traveling isn't new to me when it comes to working with my father. Traveling has taken me all the way to California, to as close as a couple of minutes way from our home in Wisconsin.

109

The location in Illinois is a little less than two hours away. My father and I become regulars at the hotel to the point the staff knows us by name and greet us every time we arrive and depart. The time there is spent training an accounting company during the days and getting more work done in the hotel room at night. We continue to carry out that routine every trip we make.

One of the strongest realizations comes to me while working down here. All of the employees we are training are older individuals in business suits working in their careers jobs. To most sixteen-year-olds, this would appear to be intimidating and uncomfortable. For me, it is the complete opposite. I have a lot of self-confidence and comfort working with the employees my father is training. But, when it comes to peers my age, especially at school, I lack that confidence. I can talk to a complete stranger at one of these conferences and carry on a meaningful conversation, but I am afraid to talk to someone next to me who's been in my class all semester long.

This inability to socialize with peers my age compared to complete strangers makes me feel as if I didn't belong at school. The whole situation creates even more social anxiety in me. I am supposed to be building peer relationships at school; making friends and creating memories of a lifetime. The only memories I am making are flashback pictures of empty vodka bottles, suicidal thoughts, failed relationships, poor academic studies, and the misery of living with type one diabetes.

Doing all of the business work is a positive distraction, but it doesn't take long for some of the other parts of life to creep in here and there. The compulsive thinking and continued search for a way out of the maze keep me up most of the nights there. When my father goes to bed, I continue to stay up for the majority of the evening and then wake up early to start again. I keep in touch with everyone while I am gone to keep them updated. Sometimes I don't want to bother them late at night, so I walk around the hotel. Most of the time, I run into a hotel employee, the big guy, during my nightly walks. He looks like a refrigerator standing probably over six and half feet tall and close to two hundred and fifty pounds.

One night as I am strolling around the hotel, thinking about my life, I come to the conclusion that I am sick and tired of how my life is going. I don't want to be this alcohol using, suicidal, depressed, fearing social interaction person anymore. This way of living is creating pain and misery, and I don't want any more of it. Before, these thoughts led me to thinking about ending my life or covering them up with alcohol. This time it isn't about ending my life, but wanting to make a change. *But, how can I change when I have a chronic illness I have to live with?*

I look out the window of the hotel lobby doors and notice it is raining. The big guy is talking to another guest, and I decide to take a seat. I continue to stare out the window and before I know it the big guy is standing right next to me. At first, he doesn't say anything and just stands there. And then a conversation between the two of us breaks out.

"What's up with you man?" the big guys asks.

"What do you mean?" I ask. Acting like I have no clue what he's talking about it.

"I've been seeing you and your pops around here for quite a while now. We talk. You do your thing. I see you walking around in between everything and being all happy and what not." He pauses for a few seconds. "But then late at night I see you down here or walking in circles on your floor, or just sitting looking out over the balcony and that person seems different."

"Wow," I said. I didn't think he would notice all of that.

"Seems like you got a lot going on in the there." And he nods towards my head.

"Yeah you could say that. It's different when I am here than when I am back home."

"It's different or you are different?" He suggests.

"What are you trying to say?"

"Let me tell you a story. When I started out here, it was about clocking in and collecting a check. Do work and get money. It's what I needed. But working in a hotel, you have your fair share of people coming in day after day. Some are the nicest people I have ever met, like you" he says followed by a smile. "And then, there are some complete fools."

"After some time I started noticing that with each person coming in I began to find it harder to want to be friendly and greet people. Started putting fake smiles on and the days began to drag on and on. I started contemplating how long I could take working here and be thinking of just saying forget it and quitting. But, something stopped me, and I told myself if I quit I could run into another job where the same thing would happen."

"So what did you do?" I asked. "You're still here."

"I am indeed. You see, the job didn't change. But I did. I got tired of it man. Going day by day feeling less excited about working and feeling crappier about it. I didn't like how I was and what I was doing. So from then on out I decided I was sick and tired of it and needed to do something. No matter who walks through these doors, I know that I can choose to be friendly, polite, and helpful. I can't control who comes in through those doors, but I can control how my attitude and my choices are when those people do."

I didn't know how to respond.

"I know you are sick and tired of something. I can see it. The same look I had on my face. I saw it in the mirror every morning for a while."

He told me part of his story, so I decide to open up and tell him a part of mine. "I'm sick and tired of being a type one diabetic."

"That's tough man," the big guy says. "Especially for a youngster. But, you can't change the diabetes. Hard to accept, but that's the truth." As funny as he is at times I can hear and see the seriousness coming out of his voice.

"Besides. I only talk to cool people. So even though you have diabetes, it's pretty cool talking to you all these times." And with that remark we both laugh. To say the big buy got my mind going would be a complete understatement. He could have ignored me all these times and had no obligation to carry on a conversation like that. But he did, and I remember everything he told me.

When we stopped working there for the month, me and the big guy shook hands and departed. I thanked him for everything and went on my way. That was the last time I ever saw him. Years have passed and so has time. But, what the big guy said to me that night at two o'clock in the morning is something I remind myself over and over again. I continue to replay over in my mind what he told me. Even though he is gone, his words will stick with me forever.

Because after that conversation I returned to my hotel room, went to bed, did not have any nightmares, and actually woke up feeling refreshed. I woke up feeling sick and tired of the life I have been living, and it's one of the greatest feelings when you open yourself up and acknowledge the need to make a change.

CHAPTER 12

Wishing and Wanting

"Every self must make its own discoveries because no one can so well understand a thing and make it his own when learnt from another as when it is discovered for himself."

Quote Inspired by Descartes

Every second I spend walking through the hotel is spent thinking; not one is spent sleeping. Of course, my compulsive thinking is at its best again. This time it is different than before. After that conversation with the big guy, the thoughts and feelings going through my mind this time aren't the same. Before it is thoughts and feelings of hatred, anger, depression, sadness, guilt, and other negative emotions that continue to tear me up inside. After that conversation, my time is spent thinking about everything I wish I had at this moment.

Doing this helps me see what I need and what I don't need, and what I want and what I don't want. I start at the beginning of when it all happened until where I stand right now in the hotel lobby. To go back to the beginning, I have to think a couple years back in a room where it all began.

Going back to this point in time I woke up with the news that changed how I will look at my life. Not only look at my life, but understand the way life was changing. It's cold in this room, and my feet are naked without my socks. I am not wearing a shirt either, only a gown draping over my motionless body with monitors taped to my chest. I try speaking, but I can't so my eyes became my voice and observation as I try to understand what has recently happened. I'm back in the hospital room, after my near death experience.

When it comes to my diabetes, there are so many things I wish I had. Obviously, I wish I would never have been diagnosed or the next best wish would have been an immediate cure available in that hospital room. This wish came up in a conversation a couple days later with my psychologist.

"Let us talk about your health condition," he says in a guiding way.

"Why?" I ask, wanting to avoid the topic altogether.

"Because we haven't talked about it at all."

"I thought this was about the things I want to talk about it."

"Oh, it is. However, sometimes we need to talk about some of the things we aren't yet comfortable talking about. Things we are even in denial about."

"Is that what you think?" I ask. "Do you think I am in denial over the condition of my diabetes?"

"Not exactly" he responds. "I think there is more to it then you talk about. How are you doing with the diabetes?"

"It could be better," I say. I don't talk about all the neglecting and self-destructing behaviors that I have done to deal with my health.

"That's not what I asked" he responds.

"What do you mean? You asked how my diabetes is" I respond with a confused look on my face hoping he understands that's exactly what he did.

"I asked how *you* are dealing with diabetes. From what I know, you still have diabetes, and that has not changed. And the condition of your diabetes will be whatever you do with it. I'm asking, how are *you* doing in regards to the diabetes?" he clarifies.

Completely stunned. I can't think of the last time anyone had asked how I was when it came to my diabetes. All of the doctors and nurses ask how my diabetes is doing. Sometimes friends and family do the same thing. But right now, my psychologist is actually asking how I am doing. Almost feels like he is separating me from the disease and asking how I am doing as a person and not an illness. That's the question right there where he gained my trust. From there on out I made it a point to be completely honest with him about everything.

"I'm not doing well," I say. "I'm doing horrible. It's been over four years, and I still don't know what to do. Four years of not knowing how to deal with it, live with it, and accept all of it. I can't change anything about my condition. It is what it is, and all I hear about is the possibility of a cure. And I just keep waiting to do something about it until that cure is found."

This is the most I have ever spoken to about how I feel about my diabetes. More than I have shared with any doctor, any nurse, any family member, or any friend. It feels like a weight lifted off my shoulders. Almost like a valve turning and releasing everything I have been holding back and dealing with trying to hide it from everyone.

My mind escapes for a moment into a memory of mine. In my room, on the closet door, there used to be a poster hanging up with a bunch of questions on it. The poster asked about your favorite food, colors, school subjects, and other questions. One of the questions was to write down three wishes. I can remember the top one wished I didn't have type one diabetes. The moment is gone, and the conversation with the psychologist continues.

"Tell me more," he encouraged.

"It is just... there has not been a single day when I can forget about diabetes. Every day, every single day that I am alive is a reminder that I have diabetes. The only way I try and forget is to neglect all the management it needs by ignoring finger pokes and insulin injections. I can forget about school and the social problems. With diabetes, it will never let me forget. Never." My eyes began to water, and tears are rolling down my cheeks. I look at my watch and notice it is time to go, and I leave his office.

As I get into my car, I realize I do not want to head home right now. So I drive around and put in a thinking mix to listen to. Because there is currently no cure for the disease, I start to think about what I could wish for regarding diabetes then. Instead, I want to feel normal like everyone else my age. I wanted to be able to eat four bowls of cereal and not have to worry about taking my blood glucose levels or measure out insulin and then injecting a syringe into myself allowing me to eat.

Ever since I woke up in the hospital, I was always pondering why this all happened in the first place. I blamed myself for it and at one point or another I even blamed God for allowing this to happen to me. And as I would learn the blame game only creates more frustration, problems and is counterproductive. The doctors and nurses could never explain to me the reason for contracting the disease. They explain what happened; that my body attacked itself when it was fighting the flu and in the meantime it decided to destroy the insulin-producing function in my body. But, even after being given that explanation it did nothing for me.

However, everything is staying the same. I continue to feel different as a diabetic compared to everyone else. I feel dirty, and I feel disgusting. I felt disease-ridden and lost without any sense of belonging. Deep down inside I still carry the insecurities about myself and the inability to socialize with peers my age. The treatment care and health monitoring is a mess, and the status of my health continues to decline.

Everything comes down to one fact that I don't realize until years after being diagnosed with diabetes and after everything else that happened after that. I had no idea what to do with my life after being diagnosed. I still get angry, or more disappointed, with what happened to me after my initial diagnosis. Throughout the whole time, going through treatment and medical help and understanding how to physically take care of myself, I am never helped with the emotional aspects of being diagnosed with type one diabetes. I wish someone would have said to me, "Hey, it sucks that you have diabetes, but let me help you still learn to live a happy life with it."

At what point in my life am I going to be able to look in the mirror, stare into the darkness of my eyes, and say enough is enough? When am I going to get the courage, the strength, and the determination to look at myself and face my self-destructing behaviors? When am I going to get the willpower to face up to my responsibilities and finally take control of my life? At what point do we become so disgusted with ourselves where we can finally say enough is enough? I'm at the point where I feel sick of being this way and am completely exhausted of living it.

But how do we know when we are at that point where we say enough is enough? It is like falling down the steep side of a cliff. We are holding onto a branch, desperately trying to grab on to what we have left. And every time the branch breaks we grab a hold of another one. And here we are; given another chance to change our ways and learn from our mistakes. I have played this game long enough. Each time I miss a blood sugar or refuse to inject insulin I keep falling and expect a branch to always be there. I almost hit a last branch when I attempted to commit suicide, and even then I felt I could keep doing all the neglectful behaviors.

I continue to break branches, lifelines that are there to try and make me aware of the self-destructing ways I am living. At what point are the branches no longer there? When am I going to recognize the fact that the next time it happens there are no more branches to grab onto, and begin the steep fall where rock bottom is waiting for me in a hospital bed?

How many times do I have to see the bottom of an empty vodka bottle to realize that enough is enough? How many times do I have to see a failing grade on a test to realize enough is enough? How many times do I have to see a friendship slip away to realize enough is enough? How many times do I have to see my blood glucose level in the three hundreds to realize enough is enough? When am I going to grab a hold on that last branch and pull myself up and over the edge of the cliff? I am tired of hanging here waiting for a moment where one of my destructive behaviors will lead to the final fall. I am sick and tired of hanging out here alone and waiting for the pure darkness to settle in.

I have been playing victim for too long. As a diabetic, with a chronic condition, I have become my worst enemy. Playing victim has become a comfort zone for me. Taking responsibility for my actions and taking control of my life means I have to step out of the victim role. I can no longer be a victim; I must become a survivor. Stepping out of the shoes of the victim will leave me vulnerable.

But what else can I do? I can't continue to hold on to the weak branches. I have to hold on to something stronger, something more durable. I have fallen, and I have fallen hard. But I haven't fallen far enough to the point where I can't get back up, and I don't know how long I can survive living this lifestyle.

I wish I could have grieved the loss of the part of my life that I cannot get back anymore. I was never allowed to grieve the part of me that is gone forever. Instead, I was pushed to move on and stop dwelling in the past. In doing so, I didn't move on, and everything wasn't okay. I shut down and never dealt with what happened to me that morning I woke up in the hospital.

I pray to God, or to some Higher Power, every single day that tomorrow morning I will wake up, and there will be a cure for type one diabetes. I will give everything I have to be free of this horrible burden that continues to destroy my life. And every morning I wake up I find out there is no cure. And without that cure I feel hopeless and helpless that I will be destined to live this life of a diabetic for the rest of my life. Instead of trying to understand diabetes and learning to live a coexisting life I continue to wait and wish for a cure.

The diabetes isn't the only area in my life that I don't understand. I don't understand any of it; the depression, the drinking, the social anxiety, the suicidal thoughts, or the school problems. All of my wishing eventually turns into wanting. Instead of wishing I can coexist with my diabetes, I *want* to. Instead of wishing I can be happy instead of depressed, I *want* to be happy. I realize there is a significant difference between wishing and wanting.

Since I don't want to change what I am going through, and I only go deeper into my personal troubles, everything continues to go in the direction of its downward spiral. But, when I want to change that is the first and most inspirational realization I have ever made. I don't want the struggling health problems, abusing alcohol, suicidal thoughts, social anxiety, or depression anymore. I want to get out of my maze and get away from the dark, dirt path that I have been living on. *I want a different road to travel on.*

I am finally at the point where I am finding answers to my questions. Finally, I make the conclusions, search for the answers and find the understandings to some of my thoughts and feelings. I am coming to powerful and motivational conclusions. After I reach the conclusion I want to change my behaviors, thoughts, and the way I have been living me life, I have to realize how my life will be if I don't change.

The summer goes by pretty fast again. Going to Illinois for a couple of weeks and spending all this time thinking about the past four years of my life takes up most of my recalled memories of the summer. Junior year of high school is approaching, and I have no idea what to expect it. I came into the freshman year of high school at my old school being enthusiastic and confident that everything will work out. After everything had started falling apart, I felt I could walk into sophomore year and pick up the broken pieces. I was wrong and halfway through the semester I left. I came to the new school, and nothing changed.

I am still trapped in my maze of compulsive thinking. The way I am going through the maze is different. This time I am sorting through my thoughts. Everything is starting to become apparent to me. My distortions and irrational thoughts begin to change, and I start seeing the truth to my life and what I have to do. If I don't make the changes in my life, I honestly don't see my existence lasting a long time.

After coming to these conclusions, it is obvious I have to change everything or live a life that will continue to be filled with misery and pain. For a long time now I have been sick and tired of living this life of misery and pain, and I want to that to change.

CHAPTER 13

Making the Change

"I've never met a person, I don't care what his condition, in whom I could not see possibilities. I don't care how much a man may consider himself a failure. I believe in him, for he can change the thing that is wrong in his life any time he is ready and prepared to do it. Whenever he develops the desire, he can take away from his life the thing that is defeating it. The capacity for reformation and change lies within."

Quote Inspired by Preston Bradley

Right away I know I have to start changing my lifestyle. *Where do I start though?* There are so many personal troubles to sort through and handle that I can start anywhere. Junior year starts, and my academic performance doesn't improve. In class, I spend my time thinking about how to solve my other troubles, and I can't focus or concentrate in school. Sacrifices have to be made to reach the ultimate goal of living a different lifestyle. I have to sacrifice my academic performance to deal with the emotional, inside troubles I am facing.

A week or two goes by, and school is the same as it has been. I still don't feel like I belong at here among the other students. Shortly after I get into the daily routine of school and adjusting to the new classes, I have my three-month appointment at the hospital to check on the status of my diabetes. Whenever I go to an appointment, I am never bothered by the fact that I continue to avoid taking care of my diabetes.

For years now I have been abusing my health, and it becomes a norm for me. Lying to the doctors, documenting false blood levels, and disobeying doctor's orders is now routine. If I let my ill health bother me I will only be facing disappointment after disappointment. Instead, I decide to not care about my diabetes and no matter what disappointments the doctors throw at me it will have no effect.

This appointment is supposed to be the same as every other one. There isn't supposed to be a life changing event. For every appointment they check my A1C (hemoglobin) level. This test measures my overall blood glucose level for the past three months. The doctors want the A1C level to be between six and seven. The doctor comes in with this new look on his face. Before, looking at the numerous other doctors was easy because I was doing a good job of lying and being deceitful.

This time the look on the doctor's face is different, one I have never seen before. It is a new doctor, but I can tell something is wrong. He sits down with the piece of paper in his hand with the results. His eyes glare directly at the piece of paper. Even though he is looking right at it, his attention and mind is grasping something beyond the piece of paper. His head is tilted downward, body learning forward against the desk, and his hand is holding his head up. It's as if he is trying to scramble words together to try and figure out what he is going to tell me. All of his nonverbal gestures are speaking louder than words.

"AJ," the doctor says in a soft-spoken voice, "your results came for the A1C test and your level is at fourteen." Immediately I feel my heart sink into my stomach and just sit there. The compulsive thinking kicks into high gear, and the number fourteen is racing inside my head. That's all I can think about right now. *Fourteen… fourteen… fourteen... fourteen… fourteen… fourteen…* The compulsive thinking stops, and I look above. Right behind him I see a chart analyzing the levels of A1C results.

At level fourteen my average blood glucose level is above four-hundred. This number sticks inside my head going in a compulsive manner. *Four-hundred… four-hundred…* Again… *four-hundred…* It won't stop… *four-hundred.* With my A1C supposed to be at level six (an average of seventy and one hundred and twenty), I am almost three times the amount over the safe zone. I am at the very top. After seeing the chart and thinking about the number four hundred, my mind recalls a memory a couple years back.

Before, having a doctor explaining this could all possibly happen actually never affected me too much. Of course not. I don't care at all about my diabetes. I hate it more than anything so what reason do I have for caring about what it could do to me. Years and years doctors have been telling me about bad blood sugars and A1C levels. Half the time I purposely forgot to bring my blood meter in the first place. But, this is different.

At this moment in the hospital, when the doctor revealed my A1C results, it is happening to me. It hurts and scares me because I am starting to care about what happens to me. I am scared that all my self-destructive behaviors have finally caught up with me. Instead of usually not caring and having no emotional affect, I am scared. I am more scared than I have ever been. It comes to me, deep down inside, that I have been slowly killing myself for the past four years.

The likelihood of developing health complications and the possibility of dying due to my diabetes is increasing. Everything is happening because of the choices I am making and because of what I am doing to myself. I am seventeen-years-old, and I am already on my way to an early death.

Then it hit me right here. Everything I have been trying to do to get myself further away from my diabetes only brings it closer to me. All the fighting and neglecting my diabetes is making my condition worse. It doesn't matter how far I run because it always catches up to me. For years, I have been trying everything I can to fight diabetes. Sometimes I go so far as to a false belief that I don't even have it. I thought by not taking care of it I was actually in control when I in reality I was completely out of control. Everything I have been doing is wrong. The last four years of my life has been living in a manner that is horrifyingly self-destructive.

The doctor instructs me to come back in a month to check up on my health. This doctor is also not playing around. He makes a note so that he sees me the next time and no other doctor. He also says that if I show up without my blood meter I might as well turn around because he knows how the results will be. This gives me one month to get my act together. One month is the limit to change how I have been living for the past four years.

I don't sleep a second tonight. I put my compulsive thinking to work. I know I can't do this on my own. I have to dig deeper inside, break through my pride and embarrassment and ask for help. I still feel like a burden to my family, so I am not pushing myself to ask for their help. From the beginning of my diagnosis I knew my family would always be there to help me deal with my diabetes. However, I know my friends would also be a powerful source of support. They are already supporting me through my other personal troubles.

All night I stay up and don't get a minute of sleep. I create what I call "a cry for help." The keys on my computer are whisking away all night. By morning, I have written a seven-page document to my closest friends about what is going on with my diabetes. From the start, I talk about the early diagnosis and immediately discussed the horrifying A1C results. No more lying, only the truth. No more hiding. I have to open myself up and be vulnerable to the truth. I can't hold anything back anymore and must let it all go. This is the time when I can't hold on to the secrets, and I must let go. As scary as it is the act of letting it out is relieving.

I place the documents individually in a bounded portfolio and pack them up. The main reason for writing the "cry for help" is to explain what is happening and the fact that I need help and support. I explain what is going to happen in the next month and what I need from them. Everything is laid out on the table; having to eat right, check my blood levels, take my insulin, measure the correct amount of insulin, and the overall maintenance of my diabetes.

I need help. I am tired of feeling all alone, and all my efforts to solve it on my own have failed. Right then and there I accept I cannot do it alone. I need something to hold on to, and that is the support of family and friends. I can't do it alone, and I know that. I am not strong enough, and I if I continue to keep everything buried inside it will continue to negatively affect my life.

I know what I have to do. I have to work with the enemy within. I have to stop the fighting and coexist with the disease that has established pain and misery in my life. I was fighting with my diabetes. And as we continued to fight, over and over throughout the years, death was calmly standing above us, waiting for either of us to end it. Death doesn't care, and it wouldn't matter if I were the one to do it or if the diabetes is going to be the one to finish it off. I have to make a relationship with my enemy to survive. Without a coexisting life, I am sure to suffer throughout the years because of the pain diabetes will cause.

Within a month's time I know I can't change everything about my health and create perfect harmony. I accept the fact that I can't have perfect health. I must try though. I must prove that I can do something right and do what I can to take care of myself. I must do something to get rid of the disgusting feeling I have about being diabetic. Either way, I want to walk back in there with a feeling that people will see what I did and say I cared about my life.

Instead of looking at the long-term goal of a healthy life with diabetes I need to take small steps. If I look at the long-term only I will forget, or possibly misplace, some of the small steps that lead up to the overall picture. I focus my attention on the short-term and keep the long-term goal in my sight. Living with diabetes is often about dealing with short-term. Look at blood sugar levels and insulin injections. Both responsibilities combined may take only a few minutes to complete. But, the fear and pain associated often leads to neglect. The short-term discomfort often leads to long-term misery.

The healthy management of my diabetes requires me to take my blood level four times a day and inject insulin four times a day. These are the time frames I initially begin using to get through one day. Instead of thinking about the whole day I focus my attention on making it through these four time frames. I keep my attention on taking my blood level, counting the number of carbohydrates I am going to eat for breakfast, measure the correct amount of insulin, and inject the insulin with a syringe. I continue the same process for lunch, dinner, and at night. By focusing on the four, small steps, I end up completing a short-term goal of efficiently and properly taking care of my health for one day.

And let me tell you something about this one day. It means more than people may imagine. To this point, I have never taken care of my health adequately in one day. At some point or another I have neglected something or didn't properly do what I should have been doing trying to take care of everything on my own. But, as I go through the first day and do everything in my power to do the right thing when it comes to my health, it is one of the greatest feelings I have ever felt in my life.

I can't do it alone. I am not strong enough. As I continue to take care of myself, I continue to be vulnerable to negative blood results and painful injections. I am vulnerable, and I am scared, and I need help. I am not the only individual making the effort to take care of my diabetes. This was my problem before; I tried handling everything on my own and was afraid to seek help.

At home, my family knows my health is in poor condition. My family, including my father, mother, sister, and brother are extremely supportive by eating healthy meals and double-checking to make sure I am appropriately carrying out the maintenance routine of my diabetes. I can only imagine how long they have been waiting for me to do this. Days, months, and even years? I'm guessing they knew long before that I was struggling with my health. This must be a relief for them as well to see me taking care of my condition.

My friends become a significant, essential, and life-saving support system. Each has made their roles within my support system. The car guy and sweetheart come along with me to the health room at school before lunch. Both of them make sure I am checking my blood level and physically witnessing giving insulin to myself. Sometimes they both come down. Sometimes it is just him. And sometimes it is just her.

"You don't have to come down here with me," I say to her.

"I want to," she says, smiling at me. "Now, what's your blood level?"

"It's 210. A little high, but not too bad," I respond.

"Let me see."

"Why?" I ask. "You don't believe me?"

"No, I believe you," she says reassuringly. "But I still want to see it."

I show her the blood meter, and she nods her head in acceptance. I know she trusts me, but I have been known to lie about my blood levels from time to time.

"Ahh…" I say to myself.

"What's wrong?" She asks.

"Nothing. This is the syringe I used yesterday. I'm all out. That's alright. I'll just wait until I get home after school."

"I don't think so," she says with a little hostility in her voice. "You are going to go home and pick some up."

I don't want to go home. I want to stay here and just forget about it and deal with it later. Having to leave school and get diabetic supplies will only make me feel different again.

"What are you, my mom?"

"Someone has to take care of you. Please, A.J. Just go home and come right back."

"Alright, alright. I'll go."

I receive a pass from the health room nurse to go home and pick up more syringes. This is another reason to feel different from the other peers at school. Instead of going to lunch with everyone else I am going home to pick up medical supplies. As I say goodbye to her, and begin to walk in the opposite direction, she turns around and gets my attention.

"A.J. wait," she says to me before I get too far. "I'll wait for you until you get back."

A smile comes over my face. It is comforting to know she will be here when I come back. It is a reason for me to come back to school instead of staying home and pretending to take care of myself. A long time now, for the past four years of living, I continuously regret my decisions and behaviors. I continue to contemplate over my thoughts and feelings. When I ask for help from friends, the one thing they put to an end is the cycle of regrets I am cycling through in my head.

The world of regrets I am living in keeps me running on a pedestal over and over again. The regrets are creating mixed feelings, confusing thoughts, and indecisiveness to make any changes. My friends push me off the pedestal and don't allow the world inside my head to continue. They change the regrets in my life to actions of changing the behaviors. They don't do it for me because they know I have to be the one to make the changes. I do the work and make the commitment to take care of myself. I can't rely on them to do it for me. I need to do it by myself. I just need them next to me right now.

For a month, I work hard on controlling my diabetes and keeping my condition at a healthy state. I take my blood and place the bottle of strips over the meter to block the number. I slightly move the bottle right to left to uncover the numbers. I am scared, and I am afraid and I am nervous. I look at the meter; 7...9. The number is 97. It feels great. Seeing a healthy blood glucose level brings a sense of relief and comfort. I take my blood again. I am scared, and I am afraid and I am nervous. I move the bottle slight from the right to the left. I look at the meter; 9...3...2. The number is 239.

I am somewhat disheartened. But I have to do what is right. I have to adjust my insulin, and I have to hold on the future vision of a healthy life. I have to hold on to the support of my family and friends and do what I have to do to take care of myself. And for the next month the numbers are good, and sometimes the numbers are bad.

The night before my appointment approaches, and I don't sleep at all. I don't want to fall asleep. I don't want to have another nightmare sending my mind back into the horror of when it all happened. Everyone knows this appointment is coming up, and it means the world to me. The anxiety is running high. Thoughts are racing in and out of my head as usual, but this time it is different. I am still in the maze lost without directions. It is slightly different this time. Questions are racing through my head about my appointment. However, as soon as one appears I counteract it with another question that isn't as negative.

What if the condition of my health is worse than before? What if the condition of my health improves? Will the doctor doubt me and not believe I am taking care of myself? Will the doctor trust me when I tell him about my determination to take care of myself? Will I disappoint my family and friends? Will my family and friends be proud of me? Did I work hard enough? Did I work as hard as I could? Will the results of this appointment make me depressed? Will the results of this appointment make me happy?

Even though my head is still filled with negative thoughts, I start counteracting them with positive ones. The maze is different this time. Instead of asking negative questions repeatedly and continuously getting lost in the maze I make improvements. Positive thoughts slowly appear behind the negative ones, and I take steps towards them. I am not out of the maze yet, but I am making progress towards it. I am starting to see life differently.

Ironically, I am not upset over this pattern not stopping right away because this is a new way for me to think. Before it was all about the negative thoughts and self-destructing behaviors. Now, I see there are other options. There are other possible outcomes to what goes on in life. It's not this or that, but there are many different ways events, situations, and outcomes that can happen.

The plan is to go to school in the morning, leave for the appointment and return afterward for the rest of classes. I know the first two events are going to take place, but the third one depends on whether or not the results are positive or negative about my A1C level. I honestly don't know what I will do. I feel if the A1C is the same or possibly worse I will drive as far away as I can.

Everyone is checking up on me to see how I am doing before I leave the hospital. Previously, I never care about going to the hospital. I have no emotional response when going to see the doctor and having them check up on my health. I lied to them all the time and did what I had to for me to get out of there. This time is different though. I made a commitment to my doctor, my family, my friends, and most importantly to myself. This appointment means everything to me, and it isn't about having a lack of emotions, but experiencing every type of emotion.

Time catches up and as soon as I check my watch and it is time for me to depart. Everybody wishes me luck, gives words of inspiration and tells me to find them when I get back. The sweetheart wants to meet at my locker before I left. I leave about fifteen minutes before class ends. She knows about my plans and already gets out of class to meet up with me. When I get to my locker, she is already standing in front of it.

"Hey you," I say to her.

"Hi," she responds.

"How did you manage to get out of class?" I ask.

"I told the teacher I left my notebook in my locker," she answers.

"Very nice," I say. "So why did you want to meet me here before I left?"

"I just wanted to say good-bye and wish you good luck."

A moment of silence occurs, and she speaks again.

"So, how are you?" she asks.

"I don't know," I respond. "Scared, worried, anxious. I don't know. This feels different than every other appointment I ever had before."

"That's because you care about your health now," she responds. "Before you didn't care, and it didn't matter what happened."

"I just want everything to work out," I say.

"We all do. What time do you think you will be back in school?"

"I'm hoping to be back during lunch."

"Thanks for everything. I don't know where I would be right now if it weren't for you and everyone else." She was a friend that did what she had to because I needed it. Regardless of whether I wanted it or not, she always stuck to her guns when it came to what was best for me. She never faulted, and no matter what excuse I tried to pull it never worked on her.

"No problem," she says. "That's what best friends are for."

She gives me a big hug and wishes me luck one last time before I leave. Before I depart, she puts a hand in her sweatshirt, pulls out a note, and hands it to me.

"What's this?" I ask her.

"Read it. Not yet though. Read it while you are in the waiting room. Are you sure you don't want me to go with you?" She asks.

"As much as I would... I need to do this on my own."

"I know you do," she says in agreement.

"It's time for me to go. I'll find you when I get back."

"You better," she says.

Every time I walk through the doors of the hospital entrance I hate it. In my mind, it is a place of pain, suffering, and I want to be as far away from it as possible. I almost died in the hospital when I was diagnosed. I almost died at the previous hospital that I was at before they even transferred me here. As soon I walk through those doors I get these short flashbacks of me sitting in the hospital bed, awakening after my near death experience.

Maybe I should leave. I'm not strong enough. I am here alone, and I don't know if I can do this. But I must. I have come this far, and I can't turn around and run. I can't run away from it now. I have to face the music and own up to my responsibility. I let the receptionist know I am here for my appointment and wait in the hallway for my name to be called. I remember the note she gave me and reached into my pocket to grab it.

She tells me something that will stick with me for the rest of my life. She explains to me in her note that no matter what the results are, no matter what people say about what happens with my appointment, I did what I had to do to take care of myself. And for that past month I cared about my health, and that's something that nobody can take away from me. She explains that she is proud of how hard I have worked.

In life, there will be times where people will bring your success and efforts down and even doubt you. If my test results come back negative, I know my doctor wouldn't believe all the hard work I have been putting in to take care of myself. Regardless of the results I know I was making a change in my life for the better. I recognized the fact that I have a problem with my diabetes, and I needed to take care of it.

I sit in the waiting room and think about everything. I am here all alone. I have no family and no friends to sit next to me and say encouraging words to bring relief and comfort. I deserve to be here all alone. I have to be the one to face my responsibilities and consequences of the self-destructive decisions I have made in the past. They don't deserve to be here. Not because their efforts have fallen short (it has been everything but short). They don't deserve to be here because they aren't the reason for me being here.

No more lying, no more hiding, and no more excuses. I have to open my arms up to the reality of what's about to happen, and I cannot deny it. I have to hold strong and believe that what I have been doing in the past month has been the right thing to do. I have to open up to the possibility that my number will be lowered, and in doing so will create joy, happiness, and relief. By doing so, I also open my arms up to suffering, pain, and the possibility of failure. I can close up again and run away. I can lie about everything and live the life I was living for the past four years.

I can't. If I fail to open up, then I will never truly know what I am capable of. I have come this far, and I can't turn away. I am sick and tired of living the horrible life filled with self-destructing behaviors and poor decisions. This is where I need to be right now, and I have to continue walking this path.

The nurse comes over and does the routine checkup procedures and draws blood to measure my A1C level. As soon as the doctor comes in I don't want to beat around the bush; I want to know my results immediately. While my blood is being tested and analyzed, the doctor and I discuss how the past month has been. I explain how my support system provides me with the help I need to take care of my health. I describe how I have taken control of my life one frame at a time and how hard I have been working at lowering my A1C level. I know the moment of truth for the doctor and I arrive when the results are revealed.

All of the sudden the door opens up and the nurse hands the doctor a piece of paper with the results. He looks at the paper, shows no emotional expression, and gives it to me. I don't look at the paper right away. I am scared to, and I don't know what to expect. This is the moment of truth. This event and these results will change my life either way. If the number has improved, I know I am capable of making the necessary changes in my life and possibly escaping the maze, and traveling a new path towards a brighter future. If the number hasn't improved, I know I will feel forever lost and destined to go towards the darkness forever.

I look at the doctor one last time and flip the sheet over. I place my hand over the number and slowly move my hand from the right to the left, slowly revealing the number. I look at the paper, and the first number is a .4. I could be anything now. It can be a 14.4 or a 6.4 or 11.4. I move my hand again, and the number is 9. The result of my A1C is a 9.4. The A1C result went from a dangerous, almost life threatening 14 to a vastly improved 9.4. This is a dramatic change from a medical standpoint. The doctor didn't even think I could have lowered it this much in a short amount of time. It can take individuals months and even years to adjust and lower their blood levels. I managed to do it in one month.

The doctor shakes my hand, and even though I still need my A1C level to decrease more, he is proud of me for what I have done. He looks at me and says, "You know there's still a lot of work to do, and you will need to continue to do it to stay healthy." I know it is not over yet, but I am going to enjoy this moment. That successful, confident feeling is inside me again; the same feeling I received when I would shoot a three-pointer back in eighth-grade basketball is in me once again. I can't remember the last time I felt this good.

As I make my way to schedule my next appointment the nurse and receptionist, as well as other staff members, congratulate me on the success. I sit in my car, turn the ignition, and immediately call my mom with the great news. When I tell her the good news I can hear her spirits have lit up through the tone of her voice. She is happy the A1C level went down, relieved that my health is improving, and proud of me for the hard work and dedication. I remembered the time

I got in her car when she found out I was thinking about suicide. The moment I called her about my A1C results is the complete opposite, and she deserves to hear the good news.

After I place my phone on the passenger's seat, I sit here as still as a statue. A tear comes out of my eye and rolls down my cheek. However, what follows the tear isn't a frown and isn't of pain or misery; it is a smile. I finally find what it is that I have been searching for the past four years of my life. It is finally here; *I am happy living with my diabetes*. The happiness is related directly to the accomplishment of taking care of my diabetes and coming out on top.

For years, I was never happy with my diabetes. I hated it so much to the point where I was doing self-destructive behaviors to try and get as far away from it as I could. I started drinking alcohol, thinking about suicide, having social anxiety and overall hatred towards life because of my diabetes. Not a single previous memory of diabetes brought happiness or joy. Everything that was related to diabetes was a nightmare, a self-destructive track that tore everything apart inside and out. Living with diabetes was the reason I was traveling on that dark, lonely road.

Diabetes has become an entirely different image inside my head. It shows me the strength, courage, and determination that I have to overcome one of the most, if not *the* most, struggling obstacle life has given me. My health is improving, and my relationships with my friends grow even stronger because of the support system we created to help with the challenge of lowering my A1C level. I left the hospital being happy about my life, happy about living with my diabetes, and not being afraid to come back. Because next time I come back I want to see my A1C level even lower.

The next thought in my mind is to get back to school immediately to tell all my friends the results. Most of my friends have the same lunch as I do, and that's where they are at the time I returned. I estimate what time I will come back and tell everyone I will probably be back around then. As I walk in, I notice all of them sitting at the usual set of tables. Most of my friends are gathered at a table with the car guy. I see the sweetheart over in the corner with some of her peers. The sarcastic guy doesn't have our lunch, but he managed to sneak down and find me.

Everyone is anticipating what I am going to say about the results. I take a deep breath, and I try to hold back the smile for a moment. But I can't hold back any longer. I tell them the number is 9.4, and the doctors are happy to see the improvement. I have the biggest smile on my face. Everyone is proud and happy. Hugs and handshakes all around. Looks of relief and happiness from face to face. I have to hold myself back from crying because of the excitement.

I don't want to leave. I want to stay here and enjoy this moment with my friends. I depended on them for help when I needed it, and they came through each and every time. I opened their eyes to my world of pain and misery and left them with the responsibility to help me deal with it. They deserve to enjoy this moment with me. I don't deserve to enjoy it alone. I don't want to be alone. I cried with them, and now I want to smile with them.

This day and the events that took place mark a new day in my life; one that will change it and send me on the new road to travel on. I know this isn't the end of everything that I am going through. I didn't forget what the doctor told me earlier that this was only the beginning, and there is still a lot of work to do. I have more work ahead of me and other personal troubles to get a grasp of and take control over. However, bringing down my A1C level is a large step in my progress to change. It also creates motivation and determination inside for me to do so. This day of triumph and success will be remembered as one of the happiest days of my life.

It is ironic to think one of the saddest moments in my life (being diagnosed with type one diabetes) and one of the happiest moments in my life (bringing down my A1C level) are both related to my diabetes. Some people expect life changing events to be miracles or large scale events. Sometimes it is the small steps that equal up to the larger goal or desirable accomplishment. Diabetes and I have made the coexisting relationship work. We have overcome death and the pain, misery, and suffering that goes along with it. No longer does death stand above us, waiting to tear each other apart and take control. We have overcome its power and learned to develop a coexisting relationship that ultimately changes the meaning of life.

CHAPTER 14

Not Over Yet

*"The greatest discovery of my generation
is that a human being can alter his life
by altering his attitudes of mind."*

Quote Inspired by William James

If I hesitate to take care of the other personal troubles in my life, I know the opportunity for them to get worse and create additional pain. Thinking that everything is solved now would just open the doors for complacency and thinking "I've got this." But the truth of the matter is so much is going on below the surface that in order to deal with them I must bring them to light. The first trouble I have to overcome is the one that could lead to potential harm; the alcohol use. The whole time, while thinking alcohol was helping me control the unwanted thoughts and feelings, it was in fact taking control and making all of the situations worse.

At first there are times of contemplating drinking and thoughts of going back to old behaviors and wanting to drink. There are triggers being set off in my head that tempt me to drink. My mind created misery and pain, but that is changing. I am beginning to see my behaviors, thoughts, and feelings in a different way. And the strong support system isn't about to allow myself to go back and drink, and neither am I.

One of the key influences that keep me from not using is I don't want to drink alcohol anymore. This want became a strong motivational factor, continuously pushing me from behind to forget about alcohol and its destructive tracks. I begin to find other ways to express my thoughts and feelings. I freely write what is going on in my head and have numerous discussions with friends.

Saying to myself that I am diabetic keeps me inside the maze of depression and hating myself. When I say I am diabetic, this makes me think that's who I am when it's not. Diabetes is not the person that I am, but simply a disease that I have acquired. When individuals start to think a disease and illness defines who they are they become trapped in this helpless state of not being able to overcome their problem.

Just because you have acquired something or have something doesn't mean it defines who you are. I learn how to separate myself from my disease and accept the idea that diabetes does not define who I am. Diabetes is a part of my life, but it's not my whole life. As I adopt this approach, I start living the coexisting life with my diabetes.

Effectively taking care of my diabetes will take care of my physical and mental health. If I take care of it, then it will take care of my physical well-being. If I don't take care of my health, it is sure to cause an increasing amount of physical and emotional pain. So my partnership with my diabetes began, and it is no longer an internal battle struggling to get along.

For years, I was always fighting with diabetes. I hated it so much to the point where I began neglecting to take care of it. By avoiding insulin injections and blood sugar levels I felt I was beating my diabetes, but it was only causing additional pain inside and out. My method of dealing with my disease became destructive in so many ways that led me to dangerous behaviors. Everything I tried to use to cope with my diabetes failed, except for this new found partnership.

I had to break down the barriers of my defense and do something I never wanted to do. I had to make a partnership with the thing that made my life miserable. I had to make a peace agreement with my diabetes. I have to live in harmony with it, take care of it, and by doing so it will take care of me.

With my alcohol use gone and the partnership with diabetes beginning the depression inside of me increasingly becomes weaker. The only areas left to uncover are the academic struggles, social anxiety, and compulsive thinking. My depression affects all the areas of my life. I am constantly looking at life in a negative way that only results in bringing me further down. When I try and climb two steps up the depression only drags me three steps down. Depression is another area in my life I don't want anymore. Depression keeps pulling me back from achieving in life and overcoming my personal troubles. I don't want to walk down this dark road anymore.

I want to achieve in school and improve my academic performance. Failing in classes or passing with D's isn't desirable anymore. I want a career in my life and without academic success I am sure to face an uphill battle. My desire to want to achieve in school became motivational. Immediately I ask my family, mostly my brother, and friends to provide academic assistance with my classes. I also search out other resources that can be useful. Asking teachers, talking to my guidance counselor and getting extra help improves my performance in school to the point where I am maintaining a B average.

Ever since I started working for my father's business, I always enjoyed achieving at something and completing an objective. I use the same enjoyment when it relates to homework and studying. I apply the same motivational technique that I use for my father's business and use it to benefit my academic performance. Not only do I achieve in academics but I start enjoying my classes and don't hate coming to school.

With everything falling into place the other area left unresolved is a sense of belonging. Since I was diagnosed with diabetes, I always felt different than everyone else. I feel dirty, and I feel disgusting thinking about having to take insulin and use syringes. I feel that I am measured by everyone else in society by my disease. Through society's eyes I feel I am an outcast and looked upon as weird and disgusting. Both high schools I attended I never felt as if I belonged and never seemed to fit with the crowd. And my diabetes, drinking, and depression led to being isolated and develop a feeling of anxiety when in social settings among my peers.

Not only did I feel different than all my high schools peers, but I felt different compared to the rest of the world. I still didn't know anyone else close to me that has type one diabetes, so I felt different. My grade school basketball teammates and relationships with close friends gave me a sense of belonging. But, when the basketball life ended and relationships started breaking apart the feeling came to a crashing halt.

I don't want to feel alone and different than everyone else. I want to have a sense of belonging and feel acceptance for who I am. Once again, I have the burning desire to want something. With all the accomplishments and success, I am having with my previous troubles I am starting to gain more confidence in myself. Confidence is a rare feeling to me because of my low self-esteem. As I separate myself from my diabetes and realized it does not define who I am, I start to realize I shouldn't assume that is how others view me.

I stop thinking about others looking and seeing a diabetic. With my drinking and depression drifting away, I become less isolated from everybody else. When my friends suggest going places and being more active and social, I don't hesitate to follow. It dawns on me that I already have a sense of belonging all along. The friends I have and the close relationships with the people who did whatever they could to help me and be my friend became my place of belonging.

Their involvement with my troubles isn't the only proof they are my friends. Everything we do with one another; hang out, talk, go to school, spend time on the weekends, go out to eat, see a movie, everything we do and what we do for each other defines our friendships. However, I know that because of what is going on with me my friendships with each and every one of them grew stronger.

I honestly don't know where my life would be at this point if someone didn't talk to the guidance counselor about my problem. Something I appreciate from the bottom of my heart. Even though it wasn't something I wanted to happen, I needed it to happen. It opened the door to an opportunity that I honestly would not have taken on my own. And their courage to do so helped save a friend that truly needed it more than I knew at the time. I don't know who to thank; whether it is a God, a higher power or the spiritual forces that be, whoever it is I need to thank them for sending these friends to me. No matter how bad things got, or how difficult I made the situation, they never gave up.

For a long time, I have been looking for a place to belong when in reality it has always been right in front of me. Even when I was attending the previous school and didn't feel like I belonged there I had my friends. Even when I transferred to this school and felt lost, I still had my friends. Even when some relationships ended, I still had friends to hold on to. My eyes opened up, and I found my place of belonging that has been there all along. I was blinded by everything going on in life that I neglected to see what was in front of me the whole time.

I am starting to take control of my life. Previously, all my destructive behaviors and negative thinking led me to lose control and feel powerless. When I started making changes in my life and the way I treat myself it becomes my life once again. No longer does my life belong to the hate for diabetes, depression, alcohol use, social anxiety, or suicidal thoughts. Life is becoming what I want out of it because I am beginning to move the dark clouds ahead of me, and create a better vision on the path I am walking on.

A New Path to Travel On

*"If you understand yourself you are illuminated.
If you overcome yourself you have strength."*

Quote Inspired by Lao Tzu, author of *Tao Te Ching*

Through personal development, growth, experiences, life changes, significant events, and observing others an individual begins to view the world through a number of different perspectives. Since I have escaped the maze that kept me in the dark for so many years, I am beginning to view the world in a way I have never seen it before.

Everything in life that brought me pain and misery are taken out and replaced with optimism, opportunity, and positive influences. A puzzle can be used as an analogy for life. Many different components and pieces have made up the puzzle. The depression, alcohol use, hatred for diabetes, suicide thoughts, social avoidance, and struggling academic performance are different pieces in the puzzle. Once I take those pieces out I have to replace them with something. If I fail to do so there will be voids left over.

I have to replace my depression, alcohol use, hatred for diabetes, suicide thoughts, social avoidance, and struggling academic performance. The depression is replaced with spending time with friends, writing down my thoughts in notebooks, and attending appointments with a psychologist. The alcohol use is replaced with spending time with friends and participating in safe and healthy recreational activities. The suicide thoughts are replaced with thoughts of optimism, opportunity, and success. The social anxiety is replaced with spending time with close friends and having simple conversations with other students at school. And most importantly, the hate for diabetes is placed with a coexisting relationship, which consists of taking my blood glucose level and always taking insulin.

If I neglect to fill in the voids, old behaviors, and past ways are sure to come right back in. They were coping mechanisms of mine, and that's what I used to survive. To take that away and forget to replace them with positive coping mechanisms would result in a complete failure, and I would be sure to go back to neglecting my health and hating my life. It is important for me to fill in the missing voids that were once filled with destructive behaviors and harmful thoughts.

The weapon that was once destructive and used for pure evil is now the strongest, most efficient, and powerful tool I can control. My mind becomes filled again with compulsive, fast paced questions again. It is different this time though. No more pain or misery or self-destructing thoughts. These questions have numerous answers and can be understood through different perspectives. These questions are not confined to the trapped maze. The questions are different, intriguing, and for once in my life I don't mind the compulsive thinking going on in my head.

These questions display a change in my thinking. For a long time, my compulsive thinking was self-destructing. Compulsive thinking constantly kept me running around in circles trying to escape my maze. The questions I asked myself continued to place me in a downward spiral of negative thinking. Compulsive thinking increased my insecurities about diabetes, led to self-medicating with alcohol to stop the thoughts, increased suicidal thoughts, and anxiety towards peers my age. However, with this new path I am traveling on I don't use a different pattern of thinking, but I change my previous way.

I know that my compulsive, fast-paced thinking isn't going away, so I use it to my advantage. I continue to use my compulsive, fast-paced thinking to generate ideas, come up with solutions, work on homework and other assignments, express my thoughts and feelings, and other ways in which my creative thinking pattern can be beneficial and put to good use. The way I used my thinking pattern in the past was self-destructing and accomplished nothing but keeping me trapped in my dark maze. Now, I have turned the self-destructive pattern of thinking to be one of my most crucial tools for my success.

For the past four years, the thought pattern inside my head was on a one-track course. Diabetes. Hate. Peers. Anxiety. Frustration. Sadness. Depression. Drinking. Suicidal. Different. Lost. Angry. Diabetes. Hate. Peers. Anxiety. Frustration. Sadness. Depression. Drinking. Suicidal. Different. Lost. Angry. The same thoughts, feelings, and emotions were constantly going around and around inside my head. They were constantly on a one-way track towards destructive behaviors and everything negative you can imagine. Now, my mind is all over the place.

Everything is falling into place. With my new outlook on life, changing behaviors, new tools for success, methods of solving my deeper troubles, and new interest in understanding the world around me, I am now traveling on my new path. I know I am not the only person going through similar troubles and experiences that I faced. After I started traveling on my new path, a larger dream has begun. Ever since I can remember I have had a deeper ambition to help others. Even when I was going through all my struggling times, I continued to provide support for others. I want to share my story; the thoughts, the insights, the observations, and all the experiences.

I notice things that I have never noticed before. My mind is changing in ways that I never thought were possible. I can see for myself, through my ideas and writings that my life and outlook on it is changing. That's what my compulsive thinking is doing for me. It helps me see things I would never have seen before and understand the world in different ways I never imagined could happen.

What do I know about living with diabetes? Let's see. First and most important is that I do have type one diabetes. It's a piece of me, but not the entire puzzle. I must be my advocate when it comes to my health and well-being. I can't do it alone and need the help of others along the way. Diabetes does not define whether or not I am healthy. My health is defined by the smart actions and decisions I make. A cure is not the only answer to living a happy life.

If I can overcome the short-term discomfort of diabetes management, I will have a good chance of avoiding misery in the long run. I have to deal with diabetes on its terms and be responsible when it comes to taking care of its needs. I cannot get rid of the diabetes, but I can learn how to carry the weight better by making better decisions about my condition. I may have lost a pancreas, but I have gained more than I could have ever imagined when I was first sitting in that hospital bed.

So what is the dream? The dream of being able to live a life where I have found meaning and can make a difference. To become a part of something much bigger than myself and help others see what change can bring to their lives if they chose to do so. Dreams without action become nothing. My life started to become more of action instead of waiting around for someone to solve the problem of having a chronic disease. The dream is real, and that's living a life worth waking up to every single morning.

Ever since the diagnosis of diabetes I have been trying to search for a reason behind my existence. I thought I was left for dead. The doctor even told my mother I should have died with a blood sugar that high. As soon as I woke up the pain was right next to me. The questioning, compulsive thinking, anger, hate, and misunderstandings led me to believing there was no purpose for living. I felt different from everyone else around me and left without a sense of belonging. Feeling lost, being different, and unsuccessfully trying to find a reason to live created the self-destructing behaviors.

But now, there is the reason to live. The reason to keep on breathing. The reason to keep on fighting. The reason to continue taking my blood. The reason to continue counting the right amount of insulin. The reason to want to go to bed at night and wake up in the morning.

I found the reason for living and overcame the previous troubles I was facing. I understood my life and the ways my mind was working against me. I struggled, I slipped, and I fell. I fell so far to the point of thinking there was no reason for living and contemplated ending it. Finally, there was a purpose and a meaning hidden beneath all the destructive behaviors.

One fact remains the same. To this present day, there has been one fact that has never changed. This fact is one of the most important and has been a constant factor. Through everything I have gone through and the dramatic change from depression and self-destructing behaviors to living a happy life and reaching my dream, one fact remains the same. To this day, *I still have type one diabetes.* To this day, there is no cure. The fact goes to show you can have an incurable disease or go through a traumatic series of events and still live a happy life.

Do you think there will be a cure? That's a question you get asked quite often when you have a condition without one. I have heard some individuals say they will find their happiness once their disease or illness is cured. Until then they describe their life as a prison sentence almost, and their only escape is a cure. There is no doubt in my mind that traumatic events and hard times can have powerful influences on the lives of individuals. And I know quite well about the physical and emotional pain associated with having a disease or illness.

For years, I would have responded in some irritated or sarcastic way. I would have said that a cure is the only thing I am waiting for. I would have said a cure is my escape from this prison of a life that diabetes has built. I was in a prison of misery, but a cure was not my escape. I don't need a cure to be happy, to be healthy, to love, to be loved, and to live my life. Thankfully enough, the advances in medicine and technology have given me that ability to deal with my disease. That being said, what happens inside my head and heart is what determines my ability to live a life I want.

Millions of dollars, countless hours, and an immeasurable amount of sincerity, effort, and hope has been spent to find a cure for diseases and illness that cause individuals (along with families and friends) physical and emotional pain. I will continue to donate money and participate in charity events to raise money and find a cure. I will continue to fight hard for a cure, and one day hope that someone will let me know when one is available. But I am not going to wait around to live my life until that day happens. So until then I'll keep living my life, and when a cure comes around I will have my arms wide open.

I cannot cure diabetes. However, I did find a meaningful life with it. I found a way to live with diabetes and not fight against it constantly. I continue to live a happy life to this day besides having this incurable disease. I found my way of living with diabetes and that is the gift that I can give others with diabetes, and others going through a similar experience. We need to cure the physical aspect of living with the disease. But, until we do we have to place focus on helping individuals live a happy life with a chronic condition.

The fact remains the same at this time there is no cure. However, I don't want to wait for a cure to be developed to find my happiness. I want to be happy with my life, even if that means still having type one diabetes for the rest of it. I took the setback of my diagnosis and set it up for the ultimate comeback. If I was never diagnosed with diabetes this book would not be in existence. Would I have the strong passion and desire to help people? Would I become a counselor who focuses on helping others? Probably not, because being diabetic created the opportunity to meet a psychologist who helped me see things about myself I was not ready to do so on my own.

Throughout each of our individual lives we will be faced with setbacks on small and large scales. These times of unpleasant experiences are not meant to be for the sole purpose of creating pain and misery, but they become challenges. They become opportunities for us to grow, develop, be creative, work independently, work cooperatively, search for our true selves, and help us be prepared to do it all again with an even more difficult challenge in the future.

The way I reacted to everything was how I became lost in the maze and continued spiraling downwards into a hole filled with pain and misery. Yes, it happened that for some unexplained reason I was meant to acquire type one diabetes. However, that doesn't mean I was supposed to become depressed, consume alcohol for the wrong reasons, or start having suicidal thoughts. The way I reacted towards my disease eventually led to the self-destructing behaviors.

We can't always control what happens to us. There are events that occur in which we cannot stop from happening. However, we have the choice when it comes to how we react to the event. I did not want to live a coexisting life with my disease, which gave little to no motivation whatsoever in wanting to take care of my health. Once I wanted that change, I became motivated to take action and decide on how I lived my life. And that's not to say because I wanted to change and became motivated all of the sudden made it easy to do. There would be no room to grow, develop, build confidence, overcome adversity, increase understanding, develop experience, or understand how our behaviors shape the individuals inside of us if everything were easy.

During the course of writing this book, I have a number of appointments at the hospital with my doctor whom I have the longest relationship to date with my diabetes. The two recent appointments are important to discuss. At the first appointment, my A1C results came back at a level of 6.5. Both of us are amazed and proud of the progress of my results. I cannot remember a time in my life while having type one diabetes, where my A1C level was at 6.5. When I returned three months later, the doctor reported the disappointing news that my A1C went from 6.5 to 7.5. Even though it isn't a drastic increase, any increase is disappointing.

Previously, my reaction would have me making up excuses to the reason my A1C has risen and lie to the doctor about the whole ordeal. This time I react by telling him the truth, and I haven't been performing a 100% when it comes to taking care of my health. After a short discussion, we decide I don't need to make any adjustments to my insulin dose and all I need to do take my blood level more and take care of my health better.

My health is never going to be perfect; there will always be ups and downs. Same happens with other areas in my life. There are friendships in life that have changed and no longer exist. Then again, there have been new friendships created and old ones renewed. When I decided to be placed on the insulin pump, there were ups and downs as well. On one hand, it can regulate my blood levels very effectively and can grasp an even greater control of my diabetes. On the other hand, I have to inject the needle into my stomach and wear it around like a pager. But I want a better control of my diabetes and improve my health, and using the insulin pump is the way to reach this desired goal.

I finally understand what it means to have type one diabetes. I understand what it takes to live a coexisting life and realize what will happen if I continue to fight the needs of my diabetes. Understanding the disease helps me get out of the maze, off that lonely dark road, and traveling on my new path. However, it wasn't easy. I didn't understand most of my health problems and destructive behaviors until after I experienced them. No one should have to go through that. We need to provide individuals who go through troubling and traumatic events the support, tools, and resources to understand what they are going through and the strength to pick ourselves up.

Life can have its unexpected events and undesirable consequences. Sometimes we may have to fall to get back up. Just because you may run into a wall does not mean you can't climb over it. We will go through experiences, tragic events, unexpected results, and some of these can lead to pain, suffering, and misery. We all have an equal opportunity to go through such tragic events. However, we also all have the equal opportunity to turn those setbacks into our comebacks.

You can travel on an easy route and still run into a road block. You can be prepared to handle the worst situation but still get caught off-guard. Life can be filled with happiness and excitement, but also be accompanied by sadness and pain. You can expect life to throw you a fastball, but it may hit you with a curve. There is no guaranty that tomorrow will come so start living today. You can fall, get back up, and dust yourself off. You can be dealt the worst hand in poker and make it the winning hand. An idea written down on a crumbled napkin can be turned into a million dollar venture. You can take the worst experience you have ever faced and turn it into your ultimate dream.

Life is filled with events that we cannot foresee coming and tragic experiences that will catch us off guard. Life is about understanding choices and making certain decisions. Not everything can be explained, nor can we fully know if the decisions we make will always be for the better.

The difference between living in the horror that I created and the heaven that I now live in is the choice that I made. There was a burning desire, an uncontrollable want that drove me to wanting to live a better life than the one I was living. I escaped the dark, depressing maze that my mind was trapped in. I was lost for years and didn't know how to find my way out. But certain events, situations, inspirational people, and decisions I made ended up helping me escape the maze I created. I made the choice to change the way I was living and follow the ultimate dream.

Would I rather be a dead person or a living diabetic? This question stirred around deep down inside of me for years. Death seemed simple. Living a long life appeared impossible and torturous. The decision of death and living was nothing sure of easy. I struggled daily to find the answer to which would set the stage for the meaning of my life. In the end, choosing death would have been a final answer with no real solution.

Choosing life was a solution and deciding to accept diabetes as a part of me was not easy. Trials and triumphs occurred where I questioned whether or not I was going ever truly to make it. The only way I could find out was making the choice to move forward and find out for myself. Choosing death would not have given me anything I would have ever wanted. Choosing life and the life of a diabetic gave me the chance to experience something I never thought I could live to accomplish; my dreams.

I used to think my story was all about what happened to me that day I was diagnosed with type one diabetes. It may have truly started there, but the power of the story flourished in everything that came to follow. And that's my story that could only be achieved through a determination to keep living. We cannot always control what happens to us. But our story will be defined and told by how we choose to live it.

Epilogue

The alarm goes off at 3am. Sleeping the night before was not the best. No, it wasn't because of the flashbacks or nightmares. I have been fortunate enough where those have ceased to occur for many years now. Last night's sleep was mostly interrupted due to excitement and some anxiety about this morning. I got out of bed, as every else did in both hotel rooms we occupied and began to get ready. Right away, I begin to change into my clothes in preparation for the run this morning.

This time is different. More meaning. A bigger challenge. A dream to accomplish is waiting for me this morning. Something I never thought I could do years ago when I thought dreams were a waste because diabetes wouldn't allow me to get there. Accomplishing this would be something I felt for so long was unattainable and even worse, something that as a diabetic I wasn't worthy of reaching.

I put on my clothes and double checked everything. I review the course map and identify all the aid stations along the way. Pinned to my shorts I have gels ready for every forty-five minutes I anticipate actively running on this course and keep three extras on me in case my blood sugar decides to drop suddenly. Instead of complaining about the extra gels to carry I tell myself if I want to finish this run diabetes has to come with me. And if diabetes needs more sugar along the way then gels will be the answer. I tell myself that if I feel my diabetes is in danger I will stop at the identified aid stations and instead of trying to be strong and push ahead I need to be smart and take care of my diabetes before going forward.

Nerves and excitement are running in and out of my mind and body as everyone packs up everything we need and head out the door to the buses waiting. The smell of this place hits me every time like a wave of comfort entering my body. It brings back positive memories of a happy childhood and even ones that have carried through adulthood. We get to the buses and drive alongside all the familiar scenes. I see the resorts, the park entrances, the short glimpse of the rides through the top of the tree lines, and the downtown area. I could not think of any other place in the world where I would want to accomplish this dream then right here.

We arrive with all the runners to the entrance area. So many people. So many supporters. So many runners. Could there be another diabetic out there? Either way I am here, and I belong here with everyone else. The bathroom stops, last minute talks, excitement from the music and post party announcements are finishing up, and it is time to move on. I take off my lucky sweatpants and sweatshirt and place them into the clear plastic bag.

I pull out my blood meter and check my blood sugar one more time before putting it in the bag. No more hiding in bathrooms stalls or other places to do it or secretly. No embarrassment or fear of doing it right here in front of whoever is around. I take off my insulin pump, wrap it up to protect it, and place it along with everything else. This will be one of the longest times I go without having my insulin pump attached to me.

Handshakes, hugs, kisses, and fist bumps are handed out before we head to the start line. The supporters are here to yell, cheer, wave, and ultimately just be there so we know this is not something we have to do alone. I know they are here to support this event, but ultimately I know they are here to support everything I do. There are some supporters who cannot come here, but I know their encouragement and help carries far beyond what I can plainly see in front of me. As much as I would love for everyone to be a part of this with me I know that this is something I also need to do for myself.

Making my way to the corrals is always a moment of recognizing there is no stopping now. I am here to do this, and there is no turning around. I know I didn't get this far with my diabetes and my life by going backward. Ultimately, I had to keep pushing forward and accepting some of the challenges and difficulties that were along the way. But there are still some doubts. Dealing with what is going inside your head for hours of running will challenge you more than the physical aspect. My brother is ahead of me, my brother-in-law is next to me, my mother is behind me, my sister and girlfriend are waiting for me, and my father is tracking me. But most importantly everyone single one of my supporters is with me.

The countdown begins as fireworks and music fill the morning sky as far as the eye can see. As corral and corral get announced, I know mine is coming up. All of the sudden the announcers make the one minute mark before it is time for me to cross the line. The fireworks go off and the run begins. All the excitement immediately begins as I take my first steps throughout the course. Right away, I'm feeling a sense of comfort and security as I make my way from mile to mile. This is not about as finishing as fast as I can. This is not about trying to be the number one runner. This is about running but at the same time it's more than just running.

I make my way through the course that is filled with so many familiar surroundings. I enter the kingdom where magic is made and through the main street where I remember going in and having my parents buy me books about drawing characters. I pass a mountain located in space and make my way around to a wild ride featuring a toad. In the far corner, I can see where a train roars like thunder and right next to it is a mountain filled with plenty of splashes. Behind me, I can see a mansion filled with haunted guests who never check out.

So many memories of pure happiness keep flooding my mind as my body is pushing to keep going forward. I finally make my way to go underneath an enchanted castle where plenty of princesses are known to reside. As I leave the entrance of the castle, I stop for a moment and look to see what is on the horizon. Leaving the castle, and passing through the main street, sits the back of the train station.

The very same train station where years ago I stood in front of it with my father, sister, and brother with my mother holding a camera. The very same place where the picture was taken that sat on the corner of my father's desk. The very same picture I saw at the moment where I almost decided to take my life because of everything diabetes has done to me. I stand here now, in this brief moment, remembering how much I wanted to be the kid again who was happy and healthy. As soon as the reality of being in the race hits me I am extremely blessed and grateful to know that I am the person who is happy and healthy that I ultimately dreamed of.

My breathing became difficult for a few moments as I had to hold myself back from crying. It was hard not to as the flood of emotions was passing through me at the same time my body was trying to regulate my breathing. My running pace slowed down, but this is a moment I would not have wanted to miss for the entire world. I think back of how running almost became a means for me to end the pain. I almost gave up on life on a treadmill that day, but now I am here fighting for each breath to keep on living. I said goodbye to that scene and kept moving forward; knowing that image is forever with me.

I snaked my way through the rest of the kingdom and left it crossing the sea where it was known to have quite the pirate's life. More resorts, more parks, and more attractions filled the path. We ran through pathways and roads that featured characters and animals from all over. Parts of the course were rough with nothing but a straight destination and less visual distractions. When those times came, I had to deal with more and more of what was going on from ear to ear inside my head. Thoughts of doubts, disbelief, and even concern crept in easier when you are having nothing but yourself to deal with.

Everything about my health seems to be in good check throughout the run. I pay attention to signs of dizziness, being shaky, uncontrollable thirst, and frequent urination. Running for this long leaves no time to ignore concerns my diabetes may present. I take my gel packs regularly as a hit those forty-five-minute increments. My feet feel good, and nothing seems out of the ordinary besides some normal discomfort from running for so long.

Another important moment comes when I enter the studio amusement park where everything seems to come to life. Runners enter through the back area and immediately are greeted by a larger tower that screams with terror every drop. After passing the tower, we move up the street, and I see familiar stores and shops with plenty of intriguing souvenirs. We make our way to the center area of the park with the giant magician hat sitting in the middle; symbolizing the time when a mouse was conducting a fantasy of amazement.

Before leaving these memories behind I notice to the right an area that was always my favorite in this entire place. Back in the corner was the animation studio, where as a kid I would spend hours and hours watching the artists draw the original characters. I would stand there watching as these talented individuals would create magic onto pieces of paper. These were the people who gave me inspiration to all of my creativity and love of drawing.

As I am reflecting on this moment during the run it is hard not to think of how I almost threw away that drive and desire to be creative and dream of inspiring just like those artists did with a pencil and piece of paper. It's impossible now to hold back the tears and my breathing struggles again as I try to catch my breath and deal with some of the tears strolling down my face.

The tears are worth it. Fighting to catch my breath is worth it. Pushing forward and running is worth it. Everything I need to do to keep going forward in a direction that motivates me and drives me to be a better person is worth the sacrifice and tough times. Being self-destructive and full of hate does not deserve that effort, that desire, and that fight. These are the thoughts I have in my head as I reset myself, take deep breaths and keep running.

I left the studio area and made my way to one final stop around the world where I was able to run through countries and cultures galore. Being in this little world made me feel as if I was a part of the bigger picture around me, and appreciating the different parts of a world I want to be a part of instead of trying to hide and escape in the dark. I am no longer living in the dark even when skies are pitch black.

A light shined more than ever when the number 26 was on a final marker. I am almost there. I am ready. My dream was not far away as I enter the last 0.2 stretch in the race. I want to see that finish line. I want to see the medals. I want to see the volunteers with the goodies. I want to see my family waiting at the end. The moment came as I saw the finish line and at that point my mind goes into full "hammer" mode and I sprint as fast as I can to cross the line.

I did it. I passed it and slowly caught my breath. A volunteer immediately comes by and places a medal around my neck. I see a familiar face in all gold as he smiles back at me. It all started with a man and a mouse. Maybe my story all started with a child and diabetes. I grab the water to start hydrating and make my way to the gear check pick up. Immediately afterward I find my family waiting. A round of handshakes, hugs, kisses, and fist pumps follows once again.

Before I sit down and bask in the glory of my accomplishment, I know my dream and the real prize are not fully complete. My girlfriend kisses me and immediately goes to my bag and grabs the blood meter and insulin pump. She knows what I am eagerly waiting to do. In the past, I did everything I could to avoid taking my blood and spent all of my energy and time neglecting my diabetes. I hated it. I hated my life. Now, I am here wanting more than anything to take my blood and see what it is. Five seconds on the meter feels like an eternity even after just running over twenty-six miles.

As the numbers on the meter countdown, I feel like everything about the story of my diabetes is flowing through me at this point. No matter what the meter reads, I know I will do whatever I need to in order to take care of my diabetes. I know I have changed. And that means whatever diabetes needs I am willing to care of it because as long as I have diabetes it will always be a part of me. Not only can I accept that but I am forever proud of the fact I am a type one diabetic. The meter beeps and as I look at the screen I see more dreams come true. I finished the Walt Disney World Full Marathon with a blood sugar level of 124. I am happy and healthy; being a type one diabetic and all.

Afterward

"Everything can be taken from a
man but one thing: the last of human
freedoms — to choose one's attitude in any given
set of circumstances, to choose one's own way."

Quote Inspired by Viktor E. Frankl,
author of *A Man's Search for Meaning*

Printed in Great Britain
by Amazon